Imagining Jesus . . . in His Own Culture

Creating Scenarios of the Gospel for Contemplative Prayer

JEROME H. NEYREY, SJ

Foreword by Douglas E. Oakman

CASCADE *Books* · Eugene, Oregon

IMAGINING JESUS . . . IN HIS OWN CULTURE
Creating Scenarios of the Gospel for Contemplative Prayer

Cascade Books
An Imprint of Wipf and Stock Publishers
199 W. 8th Ave., Suite 3
Eugene, OR 97401

www.wipfandstock.com

PAPERBACK ISBN: 978-1-5326-1817-8
HARDCOVER ISBN: 978-1-4982-4351-3
EBOOK ISBN: 978-1-4982-4350-6

Cataloguing-in-Publication data:

Names: Neyrey, Jerome H., 1940–, author. | Oakman, Douglas E., foreword.

Title:: Imagining Jesus . . . in his own culture : creating scenarios of the gospel for contemplative prayer / Jerome H. Neyrey, SJ ; foreword by Douglas E. Oakman.

Description: Eugene, OR: Cascade Books, 2018. | Includes bibliographical references and index.

Identifiers: ISBN 978-1-5326-1817-8 (paperback). | ISBN 978-1-4982-4351-3 (hardcover). | ISBN 978-1-4982-4350-6 (ebook).

Subjects: LCSH: Jesus Christ—Person and offices. | Bible. Gospels—Criticism, interpretation, etc. | Prayer—Christianity. | Ignatius, of Loyola, Saint, 1491–1556. Exercitia spiritualia. | Spiritual exercises. | Spiritual life.

Classification: BT303 N49 2018 (print). | BT303 (ebook).

Manufactured in the U.S.A.   AUGUST 6, 2018

To the Members of the Context Group,
my true educators and colleagues,
who taught me to see more clearly,
hear more deeply
and follow more nearly.

For John J. Pilch and Bruce J. Malina

Contents

Cameos for Seeing Jesus
More Clearly in His Own Culture

Foreword

Father Jerome Neyrey SJ has been a leader for forty years in biblical studies and the application of the social sciences to the explication of Scripture. As a founding member of The Context Group (1990), he edited the seminal volume of essays titled *The Social World of Luke-Acts* (Hendrickson, 1991). With this background, Neyrey is also a culturally respectful "time traveler," which enhances his exegesis of Scripture and his understanding of Jesus within his first-century world.

In this unique volume, Neyrey offers a very practical synthesis of cultural scholarship on the gospels with the contemplative tradition of St. Ignatius Loyola. As a classic aid to Christian prayer, Ignatius' *Spiritual Exercises* aim to foster a deeper understanding of gospel mysteries and a closer following of Jesus. "Seeing, listening and considering in the imagination, then, seem to be an essential part of learning to know and follow Jesus." With the instructions of Ignatius' *Spiritual Exercises* as a model, Neyrey guides the imagination of his reader through carefully crafted scenarios and leading questions into an ever deeper cultural appreciation of Jesus, "like us in all things. The theological warrant for this project is clearly stated in the New Testament: Jesus both shared with us in everything and "in every respect has been tested as we are, yet without sin" (Heb 4:15). Neyrey is particularly intent to show how Jesus had to learn, to be inculturated, and that "[al]though he was a Son, he learned obedience through what he suffered" (Heb 5:8).

What makes Neyrey's approach to imagining the humanity of Jesus distinctive is his attention to cultural scenarios understood by the biblical authors, but not so readily apparent to U.S. individuals. Because the gospel writers assume so many cultural things, new imaginings are needed within this prayer tradition. As Neyrey puts it, "the cultural world of Jesus is utterly foreign to our recent ancestors as well as to us. A kind of Grand Canyon separates us." Ethnocentric or anachronistic imaginings can be refocused and recontextualized through the incorporation of insights from Mediterranean culture, the culture which is most analogous to the biblical cultures. In chapter one, for instance, a handy table of major cultural differences about social roles and cultural expectations aptly illustrates the point.

St. Ignatius of Loyola's *Spiritual Exercises* have long inspired Christian meditative prayer. Ignatius proposes that contemplative prayer be organized by four "weeks," which respectively focus on Creation and Redemption ("week" 1), and then events in Jesus' life, his death, and his resurrection ("weeks" 2, 3, and 4). To orient the imagination to start, "preludes" are comprised of historical study and focus upon a place or a person.

Following a similar Ignatian process in this book, Neyrey directs the petitioner to focus on something concrete in the biblical story about Jesus—an event or a place, or even a conversation with Jesus himself—to prime the imagination for appropriate meditation. So the first part of the book focuses on traveling and experiencing—seeing more accurately—events in the story of Jesus. The second part focuses on Jesus' words—on listening more intently—words set within an honor-shame culture that Jesus up-ends and so redefines, being more concerned with honor in God's eyes rather than the eyes of humanity. One of the important goals of these exercises is put succinctly by Neyrey, "Seeing, listening and considering in the imagination, then, seem to be an essential part of learning to know and follow Jesus."

For an instance of "seeing" the birth of Jesus in Matthew's and Luke's stories, Neyrey helps the reader to imagine the "difficult pregnancy" of Mary measured by cultural standards of the day—by considering how women were considered property of their families, how their marriages were arranged between families, how their sexual exclusivity always affected the family and was protected by men, and especially how shameful a pregnancy would be without an apparent human father. Thus in Matthew, Joseph can only accept Mary's pregnancy as honorable because of angelic intervention through a dream; likewise in Luke, because an angel reveals directly to Mary that the pregnancy is divinely conceived, ordinary cultural expectations are circumvented. As a good spiritual director, Neyrey stimulates the reader's imagination by displaying what were the high context assumptions about betrothal, dowries, and shame and honor wrapped up with Mediterranean family life. A series of probing questions lead the reader's imagination deeper into both the scandal of this birth and its honor contrary to human expectations in God's eyes.

Likewise in contemplating Jesus' words in parables, Neyrey shows how the stories often hinge on something preposterous. An incredible debt is forgiven by a king; a Samaritan leaves a blank check for an enemy; a tenant shepherd abandons 99 sheep to find only one, so endangering the owner's precious herd; an absentee landlord does not seek immediate revenge for insult and injury. Again, Neyrey shows the reader how the audience first would laugh, then be left in silence wondering what Jesus had really meant. Laughter? Silence? Riddle. In reflections on Jesus' crucifixion and resurrection, the preludes reveal the deep involvement of the core Mediterranean values of honor and shame—while Jesus is shamed in the eyes of the elites by his death on a cross, he is shown to be honored by God in the resurrection because he remained an obedient and loyal son solely concerned for God's honor in human eyes.

In my own thirty years of teaching Jesus and the Gospels, I have often remarked that U.S. Christianity all too often presents a docetic Jesus. Docetism—the belief that Jesus only seemed to be human, but was really not like us—was declared a heresy by the ancient church. Part of the reason for this development of beliefs about the man from Galilee was the tragic separation of Christianity from its parent Judaism, and from Jewish conceptions of a monotheistic God. Christianity came to share in Greek views of the evilness of the body and changeable matter. Plato in several of his famous dialogs put forward his views that the eternal spiritual world of the Forms or Ideas is the only true reality, and that the body (subject to change, suffering, and death) cannot be "truly real." Neo-Platonism was pervasive in the New Testament thought world of Greco-Roman antiquity. While the Doctrine of the Trinity explicitly and paradoxically affirms the humanity of Jesus—one hundred percent—and the deity of Jesus—one hundred percent—the paradox has too often been piously lost in favor of a docetic Christ. A different sort of "docetism" has appeared in American culture over the past two centuries as the Creedal Jesus was replaced by any number of cultural self-portraits and individualist projections. Neyrey helps therefore to overcome a "cultural docetism" in imagining Jesus, and that can only be good.

Who should read this book? While the Ignatian exercises emerged within a distinctively Roman Catholic tradition, the ecumenical Christian world can benefit from Neyrey's distinctive presentations by seeing,

hearing, and approaching Jesus more closely. Here the inculturated humanity of Jesus is brought sharply into focus for deeper contemplation. In opening up the imagination in this way, Neyrey does what Jesuits have always
done—to bring a greater respect for another culture and to express the gospel in words and images that are culture-appropriate. Neyrey becomes the
reader's spiritual director as Jesus is granted greater respect, hence, deepen-
ing what it means to Jesus "like us in all things."

In a time of deep social and cultural uncertainty, in a time when context is so low that society itself is threatened, and when lies and false truths
are so prevalent that trust withers, Father Neyrey's book reinvigorates the
ancient notion of faith in Jesus as loyalty to Jesus and his cause, which is
God's care and cause in human affairs—toward a new humanity and a new
collectivity honorably summoned into being through God's in-breaking
universal rule. *Ad maiorem Dei gloriam!*

Douglas E. Oakman

1

What? Why? How?

This book on imagining Jesus stands in a long tradition of Christian prayer. For centuries, Christians have prayed the gospel stories, imagining them according to the common traditions found in preaching, literature, art works, and the like, with the emphasis on common, popular, and conventional ways of imagining them. Since this practice is centuries old, the scenarios imagined are themselves "old," which is a relative term that likely reflects piety from 1400 until the present. These "old" scenarios, moreover, were formed at a time and in a culture which is quite foreign to people living in the twenty-first century; we live in a totally different time and place from the scenarios formed six hundred years ago. Moreover, whether imagined in 1400 or 2100, these scenarios are very distant and foreign to the cultural world of first-century Jesus. If clothing styles change over time, so too do imaginative scenarios of what we think the scenes in the gospel stories look like. Moreover, how one imagines gospel scenes and persons reflects the previous world of spiritual writers from "olden" times, 1400 or 2100. We have been comfortable with these "old" scenarios and do not reflect much on the cultural world in which they were and are popular. Moreover, most people think their "old" religious scenarios are accurate windows into the world of Jesus. Sorry, but the cultural world of Jesus is utterly foreign to our recent ancestors as well as to us. A kind of Grand Canyon separates us.

This book suggests new scenarios which attempt to imagine persons and scenes in the New Testament *in their own culture, that is, in Jesus' culture.* Far from just reproducing better and more contemporary art, we will turn the clock back, so to speak, to imagine what the cultural life of ancient Galilee was like. Needless to say, it will look indeed strange, at first. We must consciously "time travel" to a world totally different from ours.

Why do we want to do this? What benefit is it to us? We live in an intercultural world; we have come to respect the different cultures of the people in India, Kenya, Peru, and Benin. While every human being lives the same humanity, it is shaped and expressed by the culture in which that person is socialized. Respect for other cultures, moreover, has become a value in our world, a value which we extend also to the world of Jesus of Nazareth. Let's also respect Jesus' cultural world.

Many years ago, Marlon Brando starred in a movie called *The Ugly American*, which told the sad story of an American official arriving in South Vietnam with no clue about the history and culture of that country. His role in the film called for him to dismiss the Vietnamese world as primitive and corrupt. Needless to say, he made many and major errors in policy expecting Vietnamese to perform like Americans (of course, American ways alone were valued). He had no sensitivity for or respect for the cultural world of Vietnam. In social-science jargon, he is labeled as *ethnocentric*, that is, his mental default is to read another culture in comparison with American ways of thinking, valuing, and acting. We do not intend to label all who have contemplated the gospels before us as *ethnocentric,* for they did not impose modern culture on the scenarios which they imagined. On the contrary, the default has been to imagine them according to the traditions which they have learned to imagine the traditions generally based on centuries-old iconography. Of course, they would tend also to imagine the persons speaking and acting *just as Euro-Americans do today.* The hands may be the hands of history, but the voice is the voice of modernity. This cultural virus is called *anachronism*, the unknowing impulse to project modern understandings of persons, activities, and values on to peoples of an earlier and very different culture. At least we now know the viruses that threaten our imaginations: *ethnocentrism* and *anachronism.*

Why would anyone want to take the trouble to imagine the cultural world of Jesus? Would it make any difference in the contemplation of gospel stories? Would it make that world so strange that it frightens us and chases us away? Yes, it is never easy to take the trouble to assess fairly peoples of other cultures. It takes much effort to look and learn, as well as courage to admit that "my way" is not the only way and that "one size does not fit all." Why imagine differently? Out of courtesy and respect, first of all! We owe others the courtesy of taking them on their own terms, suspending our own ways of acting and thinking, and not immediately censuring what they are doing. Allowing this minimum of respect, we are finally free enough to study and learn about the cultural world of others. The other culture benefits from this treatment, as well as our own. We are then living up to the central value of American democracy, "all people are created equal." "Human rights" extend to other cultures as well. St. Paul put it another way: "In Christ there is no male or female, slave or free, Judean or Gentile" (Gal 3:28). All cultural identity and status markers are not important before the Christ and his God, who is often described as "inclusive" and "impartial." We are 100% alike, yet 100% different. It is the "differences" we want to learn.

What sort of pedigree does this approach have? We are all immunized by commercials touting a product as "New! Improved!" only to read later how these claims were debunked. But in regard to learning about the cultural world of Jesus, we are on solid ground, approved by the major organizations of biblical scholarship (The Catholic Biblical Association and The Society of Biblical Literature). Scholars doing this have regularly had their papers accepted for public presentation at the conventions of these groups, and within them their network of like-minded scholars has enjoyed a special place on the programs of the conventions of these groups. These scholars have regularly publish articles using cultural materials in the highest levels of journal scholarship; and the library they have produced is very impressive. Not a bad pedigree. Studying culture, while no longer "new" is constantly improving with continuous research. Moreover, interpreting the New Testament in this manner also enjoys the approval of the Pontifical Biblical Commission, which published a detailed study of various respected methods of interpretation on April 23, 1993. Because it remarks favorably on the use of anthropology in interpretation and endorses the aim of inculturation, we include several sections here.

*Cameo 1: Roman Catholic Thinking on "Anthropology" and
"Inculturation"*

"The Interpretation of the Bible in the Church." Presented by the Pontifical
Biblical Commission to Pope John Paul II on April 23, 1993 (as published in
Origins, January 6, 1994).

Approach through Cultural Anthropology: "Cultural anthropology seeks to
define the characteristics of different kinds of human beings in their social
context—as, for example the 'Mediterranean person'—with all that this involves by way of studying the rural or urban context and with attention paid
to the values recognized by the society in question (honor and dishonor,
secrecy, keeping faith, tradition, kinds of education and schooling), to the
manner in which social control is exercised, to the ideas which people have
of family house, kin, to the situation of women, to institutionalized duali-
ties (patron-client, owner-tenant, benefactor-beneficiary, free person–slave),
taking into account also the prevailing conception of the sacred and the pro-
fane, taboos, rites of passage from one state to another, magic, the source of
wealth, of power, of information, etc."

Inculturation: "The first stage of inculturation consists in translating
the Scripture into another language. This was taken already in the Old Testament period, when the Hebrew text of the Bible was translated orally into
Aramaic (Neh. 8:8, 12) and later into Greek. A translation is always more
than a simple transcription of the original text. The passage from one language to another necessarily involves a change of cultural context: Concepts
are not identical and symbols have a different meaning. Translation has to be
followed by interpretation, *which should set the biblical message in more ex-
plicit relationship with the ways of feeling, thinking, living and self-expression
which are proper to the local culture. From interpretation, one passes then to
other stages of inculturation, which lead to the formation of a local Christian
culture, extending to all aspects of life (prayer, work, social life, customs, legisla-
tion, arts and sciences, philosophical and theological reflection).* (italics added)

Why now? Until recently, the unique model of biblical scholarship
has been "the historical-critical" method, into which professors for the
last century have been initiated. As its name indicates, it concerns itself
with "history," the kind of fact-checking introduced in the Enlightenment.
"Meaning" was not a common word used in this approach, rather chronology; and so study of what was unique in a narrative or a person active in
one is valued over what was common. This sort of inquiry spawned The
Jesus Seminar, an elite group of scholars who, in their quest to find "the

historical Jesus," pruned and pared away from the gospels everything *they considered un-historical*, based on their non-cultural judgment of what Jesus' world was like. "Jesus" was thus greatly reduced, since, in looking for what was unique about Jesus, the seminar judged that very little of an historical nature can be known or valued. Result: Jesus on Weight Watchers.

In the mid 1970s, scholars trained in this approved method took a turn from fact-checking to interpretation, i.e., culture. What can we know about Jesus and his world if we peer through the scholarly lenses of cultural anthropology? This discipline now has a seat at the table in the faculties of all universities; its utility is completely accepted. If "history" sought what was unique or individual, "anthropology" is concerned with what is typical of a culture. Anthropology examines diverse aspects of a culture, always comparing and contrasting these materials with data from other cultures. Yes, this comparison indicates common ideas, patterns, and values in diverse cultures, so that a sizeable database of material was gathered (i.e., *The Human Relations Area File*, housed at Yale University).

I and my colleagues learned anthropology from its sources. We consulted many textbooks used in various university "Intro to Anthro 101" courses to learn what general topics should be pursued in trying to know another culture. The Context Group then read in depth on some topics, reading professional monographs and consulting journals to give substance to their learning and to keep it current. These scholars appropriately assembled as a distinctive scholarly seminar: "The Context Group: A Project on the Bible in Its Socio-Cultural Context." This study of "Imagining Jesus in His Own Culture" is but the latest product of a member of this Group, and shares whatever pedigree this network enjoys.

"History" (concerned with what is unique) is often at war with "culture" (concerned with what is typical). The conflict, however, is misplaced, because each perspective asks very different questions. It is silly to try to decide "who won," because the quest to understand Jesus in terms of his own culture is an ongoing project. And all information is welcome in understanding it. Not a team of rivals, but a group of continuous learners who teach each other. This current book is only one expression of the continuing scholarship of the Context Group to interpret the gospels in terms of their own culture. "If today you hear his voice."

Please, this book is not written for biblical scholars, but for anyone unfamiliar with the effort to view Jesus in his own culture. There will be no footnotes here, because the author is addressing readers who trust him and appreciate that he does not need to sandbag every statement or piece of information offered. Nor will the book contain a bibliography, which is generally included to demonstrate that the author has read the right stuff. The success of the project will be measured in the satisfaction of readers who work through the material, growing in confidence with each section, and feeling full at the end, maybe with "twelve baskets of fragments" left over, i.e., interest and further questions.

How can this be done? To paraphrase Nicodemus, "How can modern people go back into the womb of history to live in a world two millennia old?" How does one learn any different culture? Slowly and painstakingly. As noted above, The Context Group began to learn anthropology from the most reliable sources, and year-after-year they study new topics found in intro textbooks. The important aim of this inquiry is to show that "modern ideas, such as "Anthropology," are reliable and necessary tools for interpreting other cultures, even truly ancient ones. We know that this idea or concept "fits" well within the ancient culture when we find ancient literature expressing those ideas and instructing writers how to write accordingly. Both the anthropologist and the student of classical literature complement each other: one speaks theory a lot, and the other verifies what the theory looks like in materials embodying the ancient cultural world. A convincing "fit" means that the lenses used to examine actually do see more clearly; investigators are not imposing modern materials on ancient cultural stuff. But, the proof of the pudding is in the eating. And so, this book seeks to feed readers with a new, but actually an old culture, just recently retrieved.

We are moving in the right direction. The November 2016 issue of *Smithsonian Magazine* focused on the cultural world of Jesus, as discovered and interpreted by archeologists—a sea change for understanding Jesus' cultural world. This article painted a very large picture by careful presentation of pottery shards, metal objects, coins, and the like. It began to put flesh, muscle, and fat on the lean figure of Jesus produced by The Jesus Seminar, because it identified very correct and illuminating aspects of that cultural world, adding where others subtracted. I consider that the value of this article for us lies mainly in its turn to a large canvas, where selected materials are sketched and relationships between the diverse items are suggested. Having said that, the focus of that article was on the world of the elites, where one would find coins, glassware, metal objects, and the like. The peasant world of Jesus most likely did not know such materials existed, much less possessed and used them. So they are never found and never become part of the cultural picture of peasants. Thus, while the article was an important advance in knowing the culture of the world of Jesus, it contains very little of the world of a subsistent peasant. It helps, but only up to a point.

How, then, do we do this? Time travel? For now, I will act as your guide into the mysteries. I am attested to be competent and conversational. I will name an event or scene in the gospels and then construct an imaginary scenario of it, describing persons, places, objects, times, etc. as one would experience them in such a cultural world. Yes, the road will be bumpy at first, with some serious action for our shock absorbers. Travelers at first will have to take a lot on faith. But gradually, travelers will discern a kind of road map along recognized highways and streets with which we need to become familiar. This map has no clock to keep time, no measurement of distances, and very few dramatic features. It will take time to travel and to learn.

One of the main characteristics of learning how to see in this cultural world is to suspend our modern passion for "facts" and "individuality." On the contrary, study of Jesus' culture presents what was typical in ancient culture, what was commonly understood or assumed. "When we read "the time when kings go out to war," this cryptic remark informs its readers that after the winter and spring rains, when the ground finally dried up, horses and chariots could ride boldly out to battle. Only if one knows the pattern of rainfall can one understand the remark "the time when kings go out to war." This is a perfect example of "high context," that is, an understanding of the world presumed by all, but expressed only rarely. One way of describing the ancient manner of thinking is to attend to generalizations, to materials deemed conventional, to the stereotypical way in which persons, places, times, and things were labeled. A safe rule of thumb is the axiom from Virgil's *Aeneid*: "If you know one (sample), you know all the rest" (2.65). Because modern thinking disparages stereotypical thinking over inquiry into what is individual or unique, we are confronted with a problem in evaluating what was typical or stereotypical thinking common in antiquity. Stereotypes were not disparaged then; they were the indicators of generalizations and knowledge about things both observed and presumed. They did not need to be spelled out. They could be presumed.

The following stereotypes are found both in the New Testament and in secular literature. For example, "Cretans are always liars, evil beasts, lazy drunkards" (Titus 1:12). One teacher of rhetoric instructed would-be orators to make much of the place where someone was born. If it was a rich, sophisticated place, then the orator should "argue that it is inevitable that a man from such a city or nation should have certain characteristics" (Menander Rhetor 2.369.26—370.12). Hence, when speaking of a specific place or people, a stereotype characterized all the people there:

> Whenever I look at the country of the Getae I saw them fighting; whenever I transferred my gaze to the Scythians, they could be seen roving about in their wagons, and when I turned my eyes aside, I beheld the Egyptians working the land. The Phoenicians were on trading-ventures, the Cilicians were engaged in piracy, the Spartans were whipping themselves, and the Athenians were attending court. (Lucian, *Icaromenippus* 17)

Remember, we are tourists in another land, not its critics; we come to learn, not lecture.

Because the people in Jesus' culture saw things in generalities, i.e., stereotypes, we note some of Mark's examples of this type of discourse. Mark introduces some interlocutors whom he identifies as "Sadducces," a stereotype that he immediately explains: "Some Sadducees, who say there is no resurrection, came to him and asked him a question" (Mark 12:18). Similarly, Pharisees are stereotyped: "The Pharisees, and all the Jews, do not eat anything from the market unless they thoroughly wash it; and here are also many other traditions that they observe, the washing of cups, pots, and bronze kettles" (Mark 7:3–4). Our task becomes direct: what mental scenarios did ordinary people have when they talked about places, persons, gender-specific roles, etc. What did they mean by "father," "mother," children," "house," "work," and "marriage," etc. Be suspicious! Our default should be, "I don't know . . . but I am eager to learn."

Let us take the common words listed above and compare our meaning of them (from our culture) with their meaning in their ancient culture. Remember the old song, "Two different worlds, we live in two different worlds." What follows is a digest of many studies of the same "words," whose meaning we learn, not just from lexica, but from the culture that used them. The following generalizations illustrate how such basic terms can only be understood only in their own culture. What they mean for us is utterly foreign from how Jesus and people in his world understood them; and what they meant for Jesus and his cultural world is impossibly different for us.

The Cultural World of Antiquity	*Our Contemporary Cultural World*
Father: the gender-specific role of *patriarch* who was responsible to provide for the family, to raise his children according to cultural traditions, and guard the females of his family; his main task: *food producer*.	*Father*: a figure whose gender role is in flux; he shares responsibility with his wife for the household and children; he provides wealth by working away from home for wages; main task: *bread winner*.
Mother: *matriarch*: another gender-specific role; she enters her husband's family, leaving her own kin behind; she, with all females in the compound, are sensitive to their reputations; her tasks are threefold: *food preparation, childrearing, and clothing production*.	*Mother*: a role in flux; maybe "stay at home" mom or in the work force. She shares responsibility for childrearing with her husband, as well as general responsibility for household. 50% of marriages end in divorce, so marriages are often conflicted and unsettled; her main task is both *nurturer* and/or *wage earner*.
Son: a gender-specific role; he is disciplined to conform to family/village expectations; his marriage is arranged; he brings his bride into his family's compound and remains there all his life. He continues the trade/craft of his father; if sole son and heir, he acquires all of his father's wealth.	*Son*: a role in flux; maleness is generally expressed in sports, less so in school. His rites of passage arrive with puberty: driving license, earning his own money, and exiting from home. He rarely follows the trade of father; he makes all important decisions independent of parents; he moves away as soon as possible; he may or may not be an heir.
Daughter: a gender-specific role, whose female tasks are the same as her mother: regard for reputation, arranged marriage, translation into husband's family compound. She remains a stranger in her husband's family, who tend not to trust her.	*Daughter*: another role in flux; she tends to better at sports and in school than her brothers. She can choose her own career, move out of the family house when she ready, and choose her own spouse. Her wealth is not limited to dowry, for she can earn and spend at will.

House: a compound of small, individual dwellings which comprises an extended family. All food, water, and fuel are brought into the compound; while males attend to food production, females are busy with female tasks mentioned above.	*House*: a neolocal structure with many private rooms; generally heat and water are brought in; indoor plumbing exists, as well as many work-saving machines. Every house differs in terms of shape, color, building materials, ornamentation, and texture. A nuclear family resides there until offspring leave to work or marry.
Work: generally done at home; for males, food production and artisan manufacture, for females, domestic necessities—both on a small scale; everything produced is consumed, but any surplus is taxed away; many children = more laborers = more crop. Cooperative ventures with others.	*Work:* labor by male and female done away from the home, on a regular schedule. Wage earning tops personal choice of labor. Workers are often part of a factory assembly line or an office team. Workers act as individuals; social relations are rare.
Marriage: financial contract between parents of bride and groom, with specified bride price and dowry. The bride follows her husband into his extended household, where she is a stranger. Begetting many children is very important, especially sons. Household roles are gender-specific, especially in terms of behavior, tasks, and social stratification.	*Marriage*: an individual decision of male and female, independent of parents and family. There is no contract or exchange, for marriage depends on "romance." Couples desire to live apart from parents in dwellings of their own choice; household duties are in flux. Some men now work at home while some women tend to work outside the house. Emphasis on intimacy and equality.
Person: socialized as group-oriented; individuality is dis-valued; gender roles are inherited and defined by customs or locale; stereotypical thinking is prevalent. Groups are predictable, stable, and change-resistant.	*Person*: socialized as an individual who independently makes major decisions, such as choice of spouse, work in the economy and political allegiance. Parental influence constantly wanes. Persons change locations and jobs constantly. There is much social mobility.

Childrearing is a good place to examine more closely. Imagine how a typical patriarch raised his sons. Consider Joseph, a patriarchal figure: *of course,* he lived in an extended family compound with his brothers and their families. *Of course,* his son was raised to be a chip off the old block; *of course,* the son will have the trade of his father; *of course,* the son will never leave the extended family compound; *of course,* the parents of the boy or the girl will contract their betrothal; *of course,* the son will raise his sons as he was raised, "severely and with a rod." Hence a dutiful father will discipline his son to be in full conformity with the customs and mores of his family and of the village. This son would never think for himself, for individualism was a social liability. The words listed above may be translated into common English terms, but their meaning in Jesus' culture remains radically different from ours. These new meanings are the stuff of new imaginative scenarios.

2

Jesus, "Like Us in All Things," but in His Own Culture

This book has two parts. In this first part I will parade fresh scenarios of gospel passages presented in terms of the cultural world of Jesus. And, as part of this project, I have divided the material into three chapters, which correspond to the pattern of contemplative meditations found in the *Spiritual Exercises of St. Ignatius Loyola*. Typical of many programs of contemplative prayer on the gospel, Ignatius divides his materials into "Weeks," that is, thematic groupings of gospel stories according to the Gospel narratives themselves. Since Ignatius' *First Week* is about theological imagination and does not require scenarios to be constructed, we pass it over. But in Ignatius' *Second Week*, he invites the person contemplating the gospel to *construct individual, imaginative scenarios* of specific scenes of the gospel narrated from the Jordan River to Jericho. The *Third Week* attends to the part of the story we call "The Passion Narrative," that is, the narrative from the arrest of Jesus until he is entombed. Comparably, the *Fourth Week* suggests imaginative scenarios about the actions and words of Jesus once he is raised. Because this arrangement is so common in Christian contemplative prayer, and since it also serves as the temporal bookmarks for the Liturgical Calendar of Christian worship, we offer it as an acceptable structure for the first part of the book.

Before we begin this pilgrimage, however, we need to talk a bit about the travel, where we are going and what stuff to bring along and what to leave home. We need an introduction to this way of considering the gospels to make us comfortable and informed tourists. I will introduce the *Second, Third, and Fourth Weeks* at their appropriate times. The second half of this book will move from specific events to a consideration of the words of Jesus in cultural perspective, the cultural issue of whether Jesus laughed, and the inquiry how he was socialized to be an observant Israelite. But now is the time to exercise our imaginations. Welcome to our tourist bureau.

Imagination in Contemplative Prayer: A Classic Example

In his *Spiritual Exercises* Ignatius instructs those praying to make two preludes at the start of each period of prayer. The "First prelude" generally consists of the history of the topic and the "Second prelude" instructs those praying to form a mental representation of "the place." Together these preludes invite those praying to exercise their imaginations as they begin contemplation of gospel mysteries. It is this imaginative action to which we call attention, especially the instruction to make an imaginative representation of the place and persons about whom the narrative speaks. Because Ignatius' own instruction is the spark of this piece, it is best to quote him in full:

> First Prelude: This is a *mental representation of the place.*

> Attention must be called to the following point. When the contemplation or meditation is on something visible, for example, when we contemplate Christ our Lord, the representation will consist of seeing in imagination the material place where the object is that we wish to contemplate. I said the *material place*, for example, the temple or the mountain where Jesus or His Mother is, according to the subject matter of the contemplation. (*Spir. Exer.* #47, italics added)

Thus those praying begin their prayer with an act of the imagination, which asks them to visualize a place (lake, path, well, village) and then to fill it with imaginative scenarios of who is there, what they are saying, and what they are doing. This same imaginative representation extends also to some of the "colloquies," that is, the extended conversations which Ignatius proposes, such as:

> *Imagine* Christ our Lord present before you *upon the cross*, and begin to speak with him, asking how it is that though He is the Creator, He has stooped to become man, and to pass from eternal

life to death here at our time, that thus He might die for our sins
. . . As I behold Christ in this plight, *nailed to the cross* . . . (*Spir.
Exer.* #47, italics added)

In this imaginative setting, we are urged to imagine what we say to Jesus in
this specific context.

It is also the case that some of the "points" for meditation instruct
those praying to imagine specific narrative scenarios as the settings of their
prayers. We quote in abbreviated form the three "Points" proposed for the
Incarnation:

(1.) *See* the different persons: first those on the face of the earth,
in such great diversity in dress and manner of action . . . some
white, some black, some at peace and some at war, some weeping,
some laughing . . . I will *see* and consider the Three Divine Persons
seated on the royal dais or throne. They look down upon the whole
surface of the earth, beholding all nations in great blindness, going
down to death and descending into hell.

(2.) This will be to *listen* to what the persons on the face of the
earth say, that is, how they speak to one another, swear and blas-
pheme. I will also *hear* what the Divine Persons say, that is, "Let us
work the redemption of the human race."

(3.) This will be to *consider* what the persons on the face of the
earth *do*, for example, wound, kill, and go down to hell. Also what
the Divine Persons *do*, namely, work the most holy Incarnation.
(*Spir. Exer.* ##106–108, italics added)

The preludes, colloquies, and suggestions for contemplation all ask for an
act of the imagination. Ignatius presumes that those praying can call upon
images from frescoes, altarpieces, crucifixes, and even biblical plays for materials to imagine gospel persons, places, and things. Because of the relative
uniformity of sixteenth-century iconography, all will probably envision
very much the same scenarios, which Ignatius takes for granted. But the
common denominator is an *act of the imagination*, which retrieves familiar
stuff in memory.

The present study attends directly to the request for imaginative representation. But it asks those praying to benefit from modern scholarship that
applies anthropology to understand an entirely different culture, namely,
the ancient, Middle-Eastern peasant world of Jesus' time. This study invites
people to suspend their conventional representations that they bring to
preludes, colloquies, and points, and to consider what was the actual life of

a first-century peasant. Some baggage we leave at home, but some we take with us on the trip.

Let us return to the *Exercises* to attend to a mantra which is heard first in the initial contemplation of the *Second Week*:

> This is to ask for what I desire. Here it will be to ask for an *intimate knowledge* of our Lord, who has become man for me, that I may love Him more and follow Him more closely. (*Spir. Exer.* #102, italics added)

As the text of the *Second Week* unfolds, the persons praying are told to "see" with the eyes of the imagination: "to see the different persons" (*Spir. Exer.* #106), "in seeing the persons . . ." (*Spir. Exer.* #114) and "in seeing in the imagination" (*Spir. Exer.* #122). Similarly, in the *Third Week*, those praying are told to form "a mental representation of the place" (*Spir. Exer.* #192, 202). The triple injunction which prefaces the meditations of the *Second Week* is now repeated: "to *see* the persons . . . to *listen* to their *conversations* . . . to *consider* what they are *doing*" (*Spir. Exer.* #194, italics added). *Seeing, listening and considering in the imagination*, then, seem to be an essential part of learning to know and follow Jesus.

What Imaginings? Conventional or Cultural?

But what imaginary representations are suitable and advisable for contemporary people making the *Spiritual Exercises?* Or to rephrase the question, which Jesus should we imagine? The one we already have from tradition, or possibly the one which situates Jesus in his own culture? They are definitely not the same. The reasons for choosing the latter are many and cogent. First, although we presume that people are imagining Jesus as a human being, that should not be presumed. All too many, even those making the *Exercises*, imagine a figure who is more divine than human. While we hear from Hebrews that Jesus was "like us in all things" (Heb 2:14–17), our default seems to be the Jesus of the Nicene Creed, who is the Second Person of the Blessed Trinity or "God from God, light from Light." While many people attest that Jesus is "like us in all things," they are referring to the Word who descended from heaven. From teaching and preaching for forty years, I fear that Jesus for many is first and foremost heavenly and perhaps human. But we are befuddled when we consider what this "humanity" means. Even in Hebrews, it seems to be window dressing for the praise of the heavenly Jesus seated at God's right hand. Those who teach and preach to Christians are similarly ambivalent about the depth of meaning in "like us in all things."

What Does "Like Us in All Things" Mean?

The source of "like us in all things" is Hebrews 2, which, when closely examined, does not tell us much. Indeed, Hebrews 2 is an extended argument that Jesus cannot redeem humanity ("brothers and sisters") unless he too is one of them. But the focus is *only on his capacity to die*. The argument begins by asserting that God is not concerned with saving angels (2:5). Then, of whom does God wish to concern Himself? Quoting Psalm 8, the author says: "What are human beings that you are mindful of them, or mortals, that you care for them?" (2:6). The psalm is said to refer only to the "Son of Man," i.e., Jesus; of him, moreover, "You have made him for a little while lower than the angels; you have crowned him with glory and honor, subjecting all things under their feet." The psalm refers only to Jesus. In fact, it emphasizes that this person is made "lower than the angels," not entirely human like us, but certainly of a status unimaginable for mortal human beings. Furthermore, this figure is subsequently "crowned with glory and honor" (2:9), again a remark not applicable to any mortal person. "Like us in all things," then, does not specifically include us mortal human beings when it refers to the person who was "subsequently crowned with glory and honor."

What repeatedly identifies this person is his *capacity to suffer and die*: "suffering of death . . . might taste death for everyone . . . the pioneer of their salvation perfect through sufferings" (2:9–10). "Like us in all things," then, refers only to his mortality, his capacity to die. Indeed, this is an adequate description of mortal man (Gen 2:17; Ezek 27:2–10), for although true gods have no beginning and no end, that is, they are not born nor do they die. This person indeed does die—like us. But Heb 2:14–18 is mute about the full humanity of Jesus, namely, the story of him from manger to cross. All we really learn about is his mortality, hardly like us "*in all things*."

Jesus, not of This World? But in Costume?

But I think the problem is more complicated, for when I listen to people, I often uncover a imaginary profile of Jesus who is really Superman. Consider the two figures. Both come from "out there," both mysteriously arrive on earth, both are reared by surrogate parents, both are endowed with amazing powers, sight, and knowledge, and both rescue those in need. We know the secret that Clark Kent, the newspaper reporter, is *really* Superman. The man from Krypton, then, is simply masquerading as the nerdy Clark Kent; he intentionally deceives everyone to accept him as the guy with the goofy black glasses who wears unfitting suits. Superman exists; "Clark Kent" is only a costume.

All too often I suspect that Christians, too, perceive Jesus, the Second Person of the Trinity, masquerading as a human being. Alas, I think that many Christians have this unexamined model of the humanity of Jesus when they read and hear the Gospels. Jesus descends from another world, arrives by mysterious processes, and presumably lives a human life. Yes, he has a male human body, although no one ever talks about his bodily functions, his sexuality, and even his emotions. His body seems important only when it comes to the pain of crucifixion. Our default belief in imagining Jesus, then, is that his "divinity is hiding" in his humanity, a masquerade, sometimes called "divine condescension." People often tell me that from his birth, Jesus knew *everything*, had power to do *anything*, and had *no limits* whatsoever, unless he chose to be that way. Stages of human development get lost in this perspective. So, nobody knows the real Jesus, only his costume. The real Jesus is "God from God and Light from Light," who is more at home in John's Gospel than in the Synoptics. Alas, one finds traces of this thinking in the *Exercises*, where we read an instruction in the *Third Week*: "Fifth point: to consider how *the divinity hides itself*, that is, how it could destroy its enemies and does not do it, and how it leaves the most sacred humanity to suffer so cruelly" (*Spir. Exer.* #196).

With which imaginative representation of Jesus should we pray? What are our options? Superman, for sure. But contrasting with that, today's Christians are heirs of the Second Vatican Council, where the Fathers spoke a remarkable word about the humanity of Jesus: "He worked with human hands, he thought with a human mind. He acted with a human will, and with a human heart he loved" (*Gaudium et Spes* 22). Definitely not a costume. Nor is this optional. Our imagination is schooled to see Jesus as a complete human being, a person with limits. How then do teachers and preachers deflate the Superman myth as a template for Jesus? What should we put in its place and how do we do this? How do we change our default?

This study invites people to imagine an appropriate scenario that is more realistic, more historical, and culturally more accurate, in short, one

17

that fully appreciates the humanity of Jesus, even to its scandalous cultural specificity. The study of the cultural world of Jesus and his times has developed in biblical scholarship to the point that it can present a reliable portrait of Jesus who is completely "like us in all things," and can offer an appreciation of the limited cultural world in which he lived his humanity. *Seeing Jesus more clearly*, then, welcomes insights from cultural studies that presents persons, scenes, genders, clothing, diet, family relationships, etc. and many other aspects of the common life experience which are part of a specific cultural world. This is the stuff to form a new scenario: Jesus *in his own culture*.

Is One Scenario Better than Another?

What does it mean to imagine an appropriate cultural scenario? How can we find out what Jesus' humanity was like, and from so far a distance? In our world of radical subjectivity, aren't my mental musings as valid as those of others? Need I change the lenses of my gospel glasses? Is there an accepted way of seeing Jesus in his own culture, limited by the conventions of his world? We argue here that all scenarios are not created equal. Some are more respectful of the cultural world of Jesus and the other people of his world, and so they deserve attention and investigation. If the task of gospel readers is *to see Jesus more clearly*, then we have criteria for preferring one scenario over others. Which scenario most closely resembles Jesus and his cultural world? By this criterion, imaginative scenarios employing cultural and anthropological perspectives are first in line for use. When those praying use their culturally-informed imaginations to represent places, persons, and things, they are drawing from a reliable bank of information. The new currency of this bank is simply superior to that printed earlier.

And the Beat Goes On

In the Nov. 27, 2016 issue of *The New York Times Magazine* ("Redemption," pp. 44–49), Paul Elie described the preparation by the actors who would soon portray life as Jesuit priests in the movie *Silence*. Because they would be portraying Jesuit priests in the movie, they wanted to discover how Jesuits acted and thought. They learned how to construct "imaginative scenarios" according to the instructions of Ignatius of Loyola. First, they began to contemplate the gospels with the aid of a Jesuit mentor, and later both actors actually made an Ignatian, eight-day, contemplative retreat, i.e. *The Spiritual Exercises*. The reporter describes the process:

> Raised outside London . . . Garfield developed his character by undergoing the "Spiritual Exercises" of St. Ignatius of Loyola. The Exercises invite the "exercitant" to use his imagination to place himself in the company of Jesus, at the foot of the cross, among tormented souls in hell. Garfield met with [Fr.] Martin for spiritual direction, and they swapped reflections. Then he set out for a Jesuit house in Wales, to undertake a seven-day silent retreat. It is not unusual for performers to allude to their spirituality. But Garfield describes the process with guileless specificity. "On retreat, you enter into your imagination to accompany Jesus through his life from his conception to his crucifixion and resurrection. You are walking, talking, praying with Jesus, suffering with him. And it is devastating to see someone who has been your friend, whom you love, be so brutalized."

To be sure, his imaginative scenarios were probably anachronistic, which is hardly the point. What counts is the phenomenon of secular, adult Americans learning to make contemplative prayer using their imaginations. Had this book existed before they began their contemplative prayer, it would have been their Baedeker or "Palestine on $5.00 a day."

3

Imaginative Scenarios of Jesus: From Nazareth to Jericho

St. Ignatius begins the "Second Week" with a theological meditation that is called "the Incarnation." First, he would have us *see* in heaven the divine figures discussing the misery of mortals on earth, and then *hear* the angel addressing Mary. Most of that period of prayer urges those praying to *look* clearly at multiform human sin and misery, so as to savor the gift of the Incarnation of Jesus into this world for its salvation. This is *a mental vision* not based on any narrative in the gospels—true enough and of infinite importance—but not one which focuses on the humanity of Jesus or Mary. So we pass it over. We chose to begin where the gospels begin, with the angelic pronouncement to Mary of Nazareth, betrothed to Joseph, who labors as a peasant worker of wood.

Contemplation 1: Watching Jesus Come into the World, Luke's Version: A "Difficult" Pregnancy (Luke 1:26–36)

We attend to the peasant ordinariness of Mary, who has probably just begun to menstruate, hence the family's concern for her immediate "betrothal." In Mary's world, women performed three basic chores for the family: food preparation (including drawing water from the well and gathering fuel for the fire), clothing production, and childrearing. The writings and art of the apocryphal Infancy Narratives describe her doing at least one of these. When Gabriel approached, she was by no means resting, enjoying a siesta, or kneeling in prayer, but working alongside the other women of her extended household. The greeting shocks her, as it should; she, a maiden, being saluted by a "male"(?) angel in her own house, who tells her that she will soon be pregnant, but not by her betrothed, Joseph. The angel proclaims "peace" and brings her a commission: "You will bear a son," not just any baby, but a male child who will be of the highest rank. This is the stuff of daydreaming: "My son, a royal child and heir of David's throne, with a kingdom that will never end?" Fantasy! Already betrothed to a man, she objects to the idea of becoming pregnant by another man. But sexual pleasure will not be the platform for this pregnancy; no, God will cover her with a fertile and creative Spirit, which has no body. The child will be particularly favored by God, a true son of God.

Mary is surely terrified by the commission and befuddled by the means of her pregnancy. How proper, then, for the angel to propose a sign, a proof that the marvelous things proclaimed are not fanciful daydreams, but the stuff of Mary's actual world. Elizabeth, Mary's cousin, who was barren into her old age, is six months pregnant with a child. "Nothing is impossible with God." The Gospel has been preached, and Mary has heard it and believed it. Shall we call her the first to hear the Gospel? The first to engage Jesus in the flesh, who is like us in all things? It is not hard to imagine all the facial expressions of this girl, her gestures, tone of voice, etc. Appropriate for a female, she is very conscious of her sexual exclusivity, her reputation.

Readers are invited to pause and digest the many cultural scenarios that will appear as "Cameos" in the narrative flow. These provide indispensable windows into a cultural world, known by all in Jesus' time, but not by us in ours. Most important is the appreciation of a totally gender-divided world. While this type of thinking is odious to modern people, nevertheless, it was axiomatic in Jesus' culture. Let us be respectful tourists in that other world.

Cameo 2: Jesus' Totally Gender-divided World

1. *Place*: *male* = out of doors: fields, lakes; *females* = indoors, household related places. For example, Zechariah offers a sacrifice in the temple, while Mary is either cooking or weaving. A *male* farmer plants mustard seed in a field already sown, whereas a *female* housewife leavens bread. *Males* pasture sheep; *females* sweep the rooms at home (Luke 15:1–10).

2. *Things*: *male* = all tools, esp. for farming, wood-working, boats and nets; *female* = all household objects, loom, vessels, cooking stuff. Animals: *male:* = sheep; *female* = goats. Clothing = gender-specific: "A woman may not wear anything that pertains to a man, nor shall a man put on a woman's garment." (Deut 22:5)

3. *Time*: *males* tell time by looking at the sky and stars; *females*, by a 28-day cycle.

4. *Bodies*: *male* genitals are outside, *females* within; *males* = strength, aggression; *females* = defensiveness, weakness.

An Ancient Stereotype: "The occupations by which a household is maintained: They should be *divided in the usual manner*, namely, to the husband should be assigned those which have to do with agriculture, commerce, and the affairs of the city; to the wife those which have to do with spinning and the preparation of food, in short, those of a domestic nature" (Hierocles the Stoic, *On Duties* (4:28.21ff). To female tasks, add childrearing.

Contemplation 2: Watching Jesus Come into This World, Matthew's Version: Another "Difficult Pregnancy" (Matt 1:18–25)

Joseph is betrothed to Mary, that is, his and her parents made a marriage contract a while ago which settled on the dowry she will bring to his household and their remuneration to her family for all the benefit she would have produced in her father's household had she continued to live there. This *betrothal* is the legal marriage, a financial contract by the parents; there is no other form and no other wedding ceremony. Betrothed, yes and so all things should be settled. Joseph has not yet had a wedding feast when Mary would finally and irrevocably enter Joseph's extended family. So he had not had intercourse with Mary, and yet he sees that she is evidently as pregnant as women are at three months. It shows! Joseph is shocked and shamed! She is damaged goods! She is not exclusively his! He proposes to do the only honorable thing, that is, to break the contract and so avoid the shame of having to raise another man's bastard. An angel comes in a dream and commands him *not* to break the betrothal, because Mary is not shameless or promiscuous. Her pregnancy is by God's power, *not* because of intercourse with another man. In fact, this messenger brings to Joseph the appropriate name for this baby, "Jesus," a name that declares his "trade" or "craft." We all know that "Smiths" are blacksmiths; "Taylors" are tailors, and "Coopers" are barrel-makers, etc. "Jesus" means that his life's work will be "to save his people of their sins." ("Jesus = Savior.") Joseph, too, hears a gospel and responds as did Mary; he did as he was directed. God, then, has removed the shame Joseph suffered and then honored him with a son whose task will be "to save his people from their sins."

Mary and Joseph belong in totally different gender worlds, just judging from their life works. Joseph is the chief figure in their betrothal and marriage: he will lead his bride to his house and his family will host the wedding feast. The bride will be integrated into the female world of Joseph's extended family. It is not hard to imagine the shock on Joseph's face when he sees Mary pregnant. Outrage, even. But he is an eager listener, and so we can see how his face and body relax, and he even become proud of this pregnancy. We can hear his voice modulate from sharp tenor to mellow baritone.

Contemplation 3: Watching Jesus Being Born

We imagine Joseph and Mary joining a large group of people traveling in the same direction, just as they did on Passover pilgrimages (Luke 2:43–45)— safety only in numbers. Landless peasants like Joseph have no animals, no donkey to ride. Moreover, a woman six or seven months pregnant cannot sit on an animal. They walk, the whole way. They presumably avoid summer heat and winter rains, which means they travel in spring or fall. They cannot walk on Roman roads (because the Romans won't let them), but only on paths made by other travelers' feet. After several weeks of this, they arrive at Bethlehem, but it seems that Joseph's kin has already arrived and now occupies all available space with their own extended families. Some traditions say they found a cave, a smart and cool choice in the summer's heat. The pregnant Mary's only task now is to network with women in the village who will assist her with her first-time delivery.

Hers was a typical labor: her water broke, contractions started, but only when they became acute do the village women attend her. First-time labor generally lasts twelve hours. The women seat her on a crescent-shaped "birth stool," which allows gravity to help draw the baby from her body (Exod 1:16). They bathe her brow and grasp her hands as the contractions intensify. Finally the head crowns, several more good pushes and the whole baby slides into the hands of the midwife. She hold the baby by the feet to help fluids drain from its lungs; a swat to its fanny brings air into those lungs. When has the cry of an infant ever been so welcome! This birth, which is just like any other, includes conventional ministrations of the women attending Mary. Ezekiel lists just such conventional ministrations but insists that they were NOT extended to his "wife," because of her shamelessness. Their absence declares that she was utterly dishonorable when born: "On the day you were born your *navel string* was not *cut*, nor were you *washed with water to cleanse you*, nor *rubbed with salt*, nor *swathed with bands*" (Ezek 16:4). But Mary's companions do just these actions, honoring an honorable mother and her legitimate child. The baby is wrapped warmly and placed in Mary's arms. Often, mothers are able immediately to nurse their infants, and we suppose that this was the case here. Nothing is said about singing, but probably there were traditional songs for successful births. In our day, we would sing a lullaby. Aren't women exhausted after delivery? When does Joseph get back in the picture? Do any of the women stay with Mary? How does one attend and assist at a birth?

Contemplation 4: The Growth and Development of Jesus ("The Hidden Life")

Nothing is said about the lengthy period between Jesus' birth and his advent at Capernaum, except the story found in Luke 2:41–51. But taking a clue from Hebrews that Jesus "had to become like his brothers and sisters in every respect" (Heb 2:14–17), we may rightly imagine various stages in his growth and development from infancy to adulthood. Infants must *learn* everything: to succeed in potty control, to eat family food instead mother's warm, sweet milk, to stand, walk, and run, to learn to speak and build a vocabulary, to gain weight and grow tall in stature. Every step requires learning, both failure and success. Growth takes years. This growth includes learning the family's traditions, its Israelite calendar of feasts, its psalms, its daily "Eighteen Blessings," and basically, its faith in the God of Abraham—*all is learned*, as is the case with all children.

To put this material on a solid footing, let us consider how the ancients divided a life-span into various stages, using their terms, not ours.

Commonly a male life-span consisted of three stages (youth, prime of life, and old age). Other life-maps make more discriminations between the stages, as in the case of Hippocrates, as reported by Philo: "In man's life there are seven seasons, which they call ages, little boy, boy, lad, young man, man, elderly man, old man. He is a little boy until he reaches seven years, the time of the shedding of his teeth; a boy until he reaches puberty; a lad until his chin grows downy; a young man until his whole body has grown; a man till forty-nine; an elderly man till fifty-six; after that an old man" (Philo, *Creation* 103–105). The most complete chronology is that of Solon, who enumerated ten stages:

> In seven years the boy, an infant yet unfledged,
> Both grows and sheds the teeth with which his tongue is hedged.
> When heaven has made complete a second week of years,
> Of coming prime of youth full many a sign appears.
> In life's third term, while still his limbs grow big apace,
> His chin shows down; its early bloom now quits his face.
> In the fourth heptad each one full of strength doth seem—
> Strength, which of manly worth best earnest all men deem.
> Let him in his fifth week a bride bespeak.
> Offspring to bear his name hear-after let him seek.
> The sixth beholds the man good sense all round attain;
> Not now can reckless deeds as once his fancy gain.
> Now see him seventh and eighth, fresh heptads, duly reach
> In insight strongest now, strongest in speech.
> In his ninth week of years, strong still but softer far
> For high achievement's venture speech and wisdom are.
> Then should the man, ten bouts complete, attain life's end
> Fate, so untimely gift, death's call may fitly send.

The point of this is to give one imagining the development and growth of Jesus warrant to imagine him in any one of these life-stages. Since all males in his world went through such stages of development and growth, we are safe in considering the same for Jesus.

We can embroider on the childhood of Jesus with reference to what we know about raising male children in Israel. Children stayed with their

STAGES OF LIFE

mothers in the compound until about seven years old, when the father took his son and began to teach him how to "act like a man," which involved much correction. The father's duty is spelled out in Sirach 30, which itself is not novel instruction, but in that culture, was a commonplace on child-rearing: "He who loves his son will whip him often, in order that he may rejoice at the way he turns out . . . he who disciplines his son will profit by him . . ." (Sir 30:1–13). Thus, a boy would experience shock by being groomed to be an honorable male, who will make his father proud in the synagogue. But at the start, he has no idea what his father wants. All is new. He has to learn everything expected of him. Lots of correction and discipline to swallow.

Traditionally sons learn the craft or trade of their fathers; and while there are no remarks that Jesus himself became a "worker in wood," he was known as "the carpenter's son" (Mark 6:3; Matt 13:55). This is probable when we consider that Jesus left Nazareth and journeyed to the one place that needed a "worker in wood," namely, the lake with its fishing boats. His first named contacts are fishermen—with boats. Presumably he labors with them and tends to their wooden boats. Presumably he shares in their catch, and so has food to eat and companionship with others. A spectator might pick one period of Jesus' development, and fast-forward through it. But remove all toys; make sure the child is working every day, all day; allow for minor injuries and major illnesses. Do not imagine Jesus ever took a bath or had his hair cut or his beard trimmed. His fingernails were ragged, as were his toe nails. Imagine the face of Jesus at three, nine, and eighteen years old. Then at thirty. Does his voice change as he grew? Did he ever throw tantrums? Was he ever moody? Could he be sensitive to criticism?

Contemplation 5: Was Jesus Betrothed? Married?

The custom was to arrange a marriage for a son when he was about eighteen years old. There is no data of this concerning Jesus, but it would be very strange indeed if his parents did not propose such a union. Children are one's Social Security; they tend their parents in their old age; they feed them, keep them clothed and clean. Isn't there a commandment "Honor your father and your mother," which applies primarily to adult children and their aging parents. Sirach 3:1–8 is still a good place to assess this. And the children will eventually bury them. Jesus will do such for his parents (but see Matt 8:18–22, where such "honor" is denied). But who would do this for Jesus? Of Jesus' marriage and children we know nothing. Is this a first step in being unconventional? What might this suggest for Jesus' emotional life, his need for closeness, and his sexuality? Do we imagine that Jesus lived alone? Was he more an introvert and did not need human company? Just the opposite is the more probable.

Cameo 3: An Actual Betrothal Contract

"In the consulship of Publius Metilius Nepos, Judah son of Eleazar gave Shelamzion, his own daughter, a virgin, to Judah—called Kimber—son of Ananias son of Somalas, both of the village of En-gedi in Judea . . . for the partnership of marriage. She brought to him for dowry women's jewelry in silver and gold, and clothing appraised to be worth two hundred denarii of silver. Judah acknowledges that he received this value from her by hand from Judah, her father, and that he owes to Shelamzion his wife three hundred denarii which he promised to give her in addition to the sum of her dowry. This is all accounted toward her dowry, pursuant to his undertaking of feeding and clothing both her and future children in accordance with Greek custom upon the said Judah Kimber's good faith . . . in regard to his possessions, both those he now has in his home village, and here, and all those which he may additionally validly acquire elsewhere, in whatever manner his wife Shelamzion may choose, or whoever acts through her or for her may choose, to carry out the execution. Judah who is called Kimber shall redeem this contract for his wife Shelamzion, whenever she may demand it from him, in silver secured in due form, at his own expense, interposing no objection. Dated April 5, 128 CE." (document from www.kchanson.com/ANCDOCS/greek/marrcon.html).

But what does the whole "marriage" process look like? Fortunately for us, a complete description of this entire process is narrated in the joining of Tobit and Sarah (Tobit 6:10—7:9). Tobit arrives at his kinsman Raguel's house and does his business. Somehow Tobit knows that Raguel has a daughter, whom he has never seen and about whom he knows nothing. At supper, Tobit asks Raguel: "Let me marry my kinswoman Sarah"—sight unseen. But Tobit will not eat until the wedding contract, the betrothal, is completed: "Raguel drew up the contract, to which they (Tobit and Raguel) affixed their seals." Then they ate. Raguel told his wife to bring Sarah to a special room where she would have intercourse with her new husband. All of this happens sight unseen. Nothing seems out of the ordinary. The sequence of wedding events is: permission to marry . . . betrothal . . . wedding feast (for males only) . . . intercourse.

Contemplation 6: Watching Jesus on his First Day on the Job (Mark 1:21–28)

For reasons not told us, Jesus leaves his village and descends to the lake. Luke says that he was "about thirty years old" (Luke 3:23), which—because nobody but elites knew their birth date or age—means that Jesus was the age of an "elder," and he is treated as such when he is asked to give an exhortation in the synagogue (Luke 4:16). He was in the last quarter of a typical life-span. At the lake, Jesus networks with certain people, namely, fishermen with wooden boats. In Capernaum, he works with two sets of brothers who were fishermen (as well as Philip in Bethsaida, John 1:44). It is not hard to imagine Jesus repairing their boats with rough lumber and stone tools. Jesus, then, is bonded to them by trade, fellowship, and worship. The brothers come to know him well enough, so when he says, "Come, follow me," they were already familiar with him and had laid down a foundation of trust. If inclined, one might spend a day on the beach with Jesus and others, watching them repair their boats and nets, share the catch, and chatter the whole day long.

Jesus attends synagogue weekly "as was his custom" (Luke 4:16). Considered an "elder," Jesus is asked to speak, during which a man with an unclean spirit bolts toward him, threatening him, "What have you to do with us, Jesus of Nazareth? Have you come to destroy us?" (Mark 1:24). Jesus responds in a way which he has never done before; he is learning on the job that God has empowered him (Mark 1:10–11) with a powerful, holy Spirit, to war against the unclean spirits. He learns now what it means to have this power and so to heal sick people. Everyone there was amazed, including Jesus. Imagine Jesus standing and speaking, then gesturing toward the approaching man, and raising his forehead and amplifying his voice. Moderate of spirit, he becomes excited and shouts back at the demon in the man. Did he learn to do this? Or, was he learning on the fly?

Peter invites Jesus to the main meal at his house, a mark of singular hospitality. Jesus has barely entered the courtyard when he learns that Peter's mother-in-law is sick with a fever—"fever" being caused by another evil spirit. Jesus realizes what is expected of him, and he "rebukes" the spirit (Luke 4:39), just as he did in the synagogue. Proof of this healing follows when the woman resumed her duties, serving Jesus and others. She is restored to health and to her proper social place. Everyone is seated in a circle, taking turns to scoop with their fingers food set in the middle of the group. Surely they licked these fingers clean. Daylight fades and night darkens. Since no work is allowed on the sabbath, with nightfall it is now acceptable for people to carry stretchers and lead ill persons to the path outside Peter's house. The prevailing etiology of "sickness" in that world was *spirit aggression;* the warring actions of evil spirits cause all bodily harm: death (Mark 7:26), muteness (Luke 11:14; Mark 1:32), blindness (Matt 12:22), deafness (Matt 11:5; Luke 7:22), and paralysis (Matt 10:8). Are any illnesses immune to Jesus' word and touch?

How did Jesus know that he had God's power to battle these demons and so heal diverse bodily diseases? Was just the sight of seeing people in distress a grace from God empowering him to respond to them? Did he experience a desire to be of maximum help, which showed itself in his touching the sick and speaking words of power over them? If he learned all other behaviors in growing up, we image that he is learning on the job now, acting and being confirmed by God. The crowds, too, were learning, "For they brought to him all who were sick . . . and the whole city was gathered around the door. And he cured many who were sick with various diseases, and cast out many demons" (Mark 1:32–34). Everyone was amazed, including Jesus.

Cameo 4: Worker in Wood: Houses and Boats

If by "carpenter" we mean a skilled artisan with metal tools, then Jesus was *not* a carpenter. Let's call him "a worker in wood." His only tools were sharp stones: sharp stone *chisels, axes, knives, sickles,* made of flint chips; also stone *hammers.* Peasants had no "furniture," so carpenters did not make furniture; all slept on the hard-packed ground and sat on their haunches for meals. Their houses were made of wood, primitively hewn, maybe planed (a stone *adz*). Scant rainfall yields small trees. Generally extended families lived in compounds which housed parents, their married sons and their children, grandparents and maybe other relatives. Within, there were as many small, rectangular "houses" as needed for the individual families living within. Together they formed the walls of of the compound. Before the gate was locked at night, whatever animals the family owned would be within, being fed behind a "manger," that is, a feeding troff that penned the animals to the back of some space. Houses likely had some sort of stone foundation, i.e., a low wall of stones and mortar; atop which slender or split trees made vertical walls, which were covered with thatch and whatever might make them rainproof (plaster, stucco). At best, a typical room was small, constrained by the length of the trees that made the roof. Roofs were laid out in a sort of corduroy pattern of tree parts, which were covered over with layers of vegetable matter, palm fronds, and thatch. It was then smoothed over with a compound to make it waterproof. In summer, the family slept up there; during the day it was the place to dry vegetables, fruits, and clothes. The roof was pitched so that rainwater would flow into a cistern below. The compound had but one cooking place where the females prepared the main meal together. Scarce firewood was scavenged by groups of these women, looking for whatever would burn to cook the meal. "Workers in wood" helped make houses and farm implements, but not household things.

Contemplation 7: Watching Jesus Engage Our Illnesses

Indoor healings are rare; generally Jesus encounters people out of doors or their families bring them to Jesus in the village square. The "news" about him spreads rapidly and widely. Unlike all other healers, Jesus heals *all* diseases, not just blindness, deafness or lameness (Matt 10:8). He heals males and females, Israelites and Gentiles, slaves and free persons—because his conception of "purity" differs radically from that of a rival group, such as the Pharisees. While told in individual stories, this inclusivity is an essential part of his gospel (see Gal 3:28). Can we imagine the variety of ages, body types, clothing, features, and languages in the groups who approach Jesus?

But moving from the general to the particular, we see Jesus coming upon a funeral of a son of a widow, who mourns the loss of her son, her last support (Luke 7:11–17). He speaks to her, "Do not weep"—by no means empty words, for at this moment "he had compassion for her" (Luke 7:13). "Compassion" is a visceral verb here, which literally means a "bowel movement," a punch in the stomach, a "gut reaction." Jesus often views scenes "with compassion" (Matt 14:14; 18:27; Mark 6:34; 8:2; 9:22; Luke 10:33; 15:20). This speaks to Jesus' physical involvement in the physical needs of these people; yes, he had powerful feelings.

The evangelists commonly remark that Jesus eschewed fame and renown. He silences demons striving to proclaim him (Mark 1:24); he forbids a healed leper to broadcast his healing (Mark 1:44); he entered a house and "did not want anyone to know he was there" (7:24); even the great confession at Caesarea Phillipi is silenced (Mark 8:30). An astute observer will notice that he is *not* pursuing fame, glory, and honor as all other males are. Such belong to God alone. His practice is to stand outside the circle, not be its center. As he told his disciples, do not try to be first or greatest; on the contrary be the last, the least, and the servant of all. He says that he came to serve, not to be served.

Cameo 5: Dreadful Health Conditions

Jesus' audience consists of subsistence peasants, wearing homespun clothing, with tangled hair and beard, split toe nails and ragged fingernails, whose diet is mostly vegetarian. Forget combs, brushes, soap, and bathing; their one set of clothes, which they are even now wearing, was woven by their females from wool from their sheep. Clothing is gender-specific: "A woman may not wear a man's apparel, nor shall a man put on a woman's garment" (Deut 22:5). As we strive to see Jesus more clearly, we can do the same for the people Jesus heals. People forty years old are unusual; living through one's thirties is uncommon (two-thirds of those born in a given year are dead by puberty). Moreover, all have health problems: broken bones that healed badly, skin diseases (which they call "leprosy"), blindness and deafness, acute dental problems, arthritis from sleeping on dirt floors, to say nothing of contagious diseases. No one is obese because of food scarcity; but many are hungry. The UN Health Commission would describe this as a "Third World" situation.

Contemplation 8: What Do the Healings Mean?
What Conclusions May We Draw?

Even as we see Jesus more clearly, let us observe how the crowds react to these healings. They interpret them as Jesus' credentials, proof that he is on God's side. Overwhelmingly God is "magnified," "praised," "given glory," as they "declared how much God has done" and "were astounded at the greatness of God." They probably shout psalms from their excellent memories. They correctly conclude, "A great prophet has risen among us!" (Luke 7:16). The man born blind forms an irrefutable argument from Jesus' healing of him. While unbelievers declare: "'We do not know where he comes from,'" he answered:

> You do not know where he comes from, and yet he opened my eyes. *We know that God does not listen to sinners, but he does listen to one who worships him and obeys his will. Never since the world began has it been heard that anyone opened the eyes of a person born blind. If this man were not from God, he could do nothing.* (John 9:30–32)

QED! Jesus indeed works the same healings and miracles performed by the great prophets, Elijah and Elisha; people do well to acclaim him a prophet because of his works and deeds (Luke 7:16; Matt 21:11 Mark 6:15; 8:28; Luke 4:24–27). Although the healings expand Jesus' reputation, he himself chooses to receive very little fame and honor, which is rightly directed to God, who in Jesus is visiting his people. This correlates with Jesus' teaching on being last, least, and humble, the servant of others.

Contemplation 9: Feeding the Hungry (Mark 6:30–44, 8:1–10)

Droughts were common in Jesus' time, so the subsistence level of peasants was very fragile. In this context, we imagine how striking was Jesus' initiative to feed *crowds*. One feeding occurs across the lake in Gentile territory (Mark 6:45–52) in a "barren" place, with no fields and farms and no water. Jesus interrupts the debriefing of his disciples because of the acute crisis facing him: "They are like sheep without a shepherd." While Jesus has a "gut reaction" of compassion for them, the disciples simply want to dismiss them. As is Jesus' way, less becomes more: a few loaves and some fish become enough to feed the 5000 people gathered. More importantly, "They were filled," something that rarely happened to peasants, to eat today without strategy for tomorrow's scarceness. "Filled," so much so that fragments fill twelve baskets. The crowd must be filled, if they leave behind any food. He does it again, now back in Israelite territory (Mark 8:1–10).

What size were the loaves? Multi-grain or bleached flour? And the fish? Small? Smoked? Imagine the surprise as one loaf, when broken in two, provides enough bread for ten, and so on. Does anyone ask for more? How did the bread taste? Did they eat quickly or chew slowly and savor the food? Do they ask where all this food came from?

Cameo 6: What's for Lunch Today? A Peasant's Diet

Grains & wheat: The diet of Israelites consisted of a few basic staples: grain, oil and wine, grain being the most important staple. *Bread* provided one-half of the caloric intake for much of the ancient Mediterranean region. *Vegetables,* while common, were food of inferior status. Of the vegetables, legumes were the more desirable, i.e., lentils, beans, peas, chickpeas, and lupines. Turnips were the food of the poor. Of the green, leafy vegetables, cabbage was the most popular. *Olive oil* and *fruit,* principally the *dried fig,* were also important parts of a diet. *Wine,* only occasionally consumed, supplied another quarter of the daily caloric intake. *Meat and poultry* were expensive and thus very rare for peasants. They ate it only on feast days, though temple priests ate it in abundance (i.e., their portion of temple sacrifices). *Fish,* a typical Sabbath dish, was difficult to obtain, unless one lived near the Mediterranean coast and Sea of Galilee. The fruits and vegetables were seasonal items, but otherwise the daily meal was identical every day.

Contemplation 10: Who Has Ears to Hear, Let Them Listen: No Attack! No Revenge!

Jesus was a powerful speaker, both in content and power of voice. To reach all in the crowds, he spoke loudly and lively. Moreover, all evangelists record Jesus speaking like a prophet, *mighty in word* and deed. Many of his remarks were gathered into large collections, where similar themes are treated. We have come to label these "Sermons." The Sermon in Matthew 5–7 is one such collection. But, careful. His audience as well as his disciples find these words hard to hear and harder to practice. Often they ask him in private what he meant; but not this time. No, it is not easy for disciples to "hear him more clearly." But try we must. It is just as important to imagine the content of his words as it is to see his actions more clearly. We begin with a large collection of Jesus' words, known to us as the Sermon on the Mount.

The first section of the Sermon on the Mount contains "Antitheses," that is, contrasts between tradition and Jesus' new teaching. The first one reads: "You have heard that it was said, 'You shall not murder'; and 'whoever murders shall be liable to judgment.'" In a world of honor and shame, when a man is murdered, he cannot defend himself nor increase in honor, for his "earning" days are over; his murder, moreover, will likely shame his family because he can no longer defend them or provide for them. *Murder is a consummate attack on a man's honor.* Jesus forbids his disciples even to act aggressively to gain more honor or to take revenge for lost honor. They may not play this game, period! Moreover, if disciples are attacked, they may not seek to recover honor by revenge and vengeance, socially accepted actions to restore honor. They may not attack, take life, or boast of their prowess; nor, if injured, can they seek retaliation, even "an eye for an eye." In the eyes of neighbors, the disciples are shameless, un-masculine, and weak—in US terms, wimps. Imagine the sour faces that look at Jesus as he tells them this. Are people shaking their heads? Do they scratch them, suggesting that Jesus is daffy?

But "anger"? Anger arises after an injury is received, which excites the injured person to retaliate. Thus "anger" leads to revenge and restoration of honor, a scenario all expect. But Jesus says, that far from receiving respect from one's peers, "anger," when acted out, is "liable to judgment," that is, a public reproach—but before whom? The elders of the town sitting at the gate who adjudicate disputes? Then in whose eyes? Far from hearing applause for refraining from anger and vengeance, the disciples will hear censure, that is, "Shame on you" for *not* retaliating. Beyond dramatic physical actions of retaliation and anger, even verbal insults will be aired in public, and the paramount insult, "You fool," will bring public shame upon him who says it. What is wrong with this picture? Everything! Behavior deemed honorable and manly in the eyes of one's peers is shameful in God's eyes. Not only may disciples not attack and so gain honor, but they are proscribed *from* seeking revenge and restoring lost honor. Surely, Jesus can't mean this? Who would humiliate himself so basely before kin and neighbors? This is social suicide.

It gets worse. Jesus cites a case where a man is offering a sacrifice in the temple, and remembers that a neighbor *has something against him* (i.e., the offerer is the aggressor). The man honoring God with sacrifice has offended someone, in public, of course, and shamed him. He must leave the public sacrifice—a strange thing indeed—and go back to that public place and "come to terms" with his accuser. The verb here is "be reconciled with," which has nothing to do with repentance or request for forgiveness. Here we need to reach into our bag of "high context" information. Jacob sought to be reconciled with Esau by *sending him rich gifts,* "to find favor in your sight" (Gen 32:13–21); David sought reconciliation with Saul by *sending him hundreds of heads* of his Philistine enemies (1 Sam 29:4). It was culturally impossible for an ancient to apologize or confess fault in public. The conventional solution was to offer some form of *material recompense,* an animal, produce, or wealth; this was not only the best, but the only way to call off a feud. Now Jesus teaches his disciples to do the impossible, to call off a fight and to make public restitution. "I would rather die than do that!"

Contemplation 11: In Whose Eyes Do You Want to Look Good? (Matt 6:1–18)

Observant Israelites made pilgrimage to the temple to make offerings and sacrifices; wealthy folk could afford bulls, rams, and goats, whereas peasants only offerings of bread and wine and small critters, such as pigeons. These were dramatically visible to all, produced olfactory delight, and even tasted good. After 76 CE, with the temple in ruins, Israelites substituted for that liturgy the triad: *almsgiving, prayer, and fasting,* the same trio which is the subject of Jesus' teaching in Matt 6:1–18. Typically these were practiced in public, mostly in the synagogue and also in the marketplace. Of course God was honored, but those who practiced them before their male peers were deemed honorable in the eyes of others, an added benefit of considerable value. This public practice of *piety for praise in men's eyes* is the target of Jesus' remarks. Not in public, but in private (i.e., at home); not to look good in men's eyes, but to appear such in God's eyes. Again, in a "high context," "reward" means *praise and honor,* not from men, but from God in heaven. Money or wealth, then, are not the "reward" of which Jesus speaks, but the respect, honor, and praise God bestows on those who eschew earthly honors. "Looking good in God's eyes, not men's" (see Mark 8:33) is a refrain throughout Jesus' teachings and characterizes his own behavior. To be sure, a studied rejection of men's honor will be taken as either arrogance or folly. The code requires men to practice public piety, but refusal to do so will be interpreted as contempt for God and treason toward Israel. Jesus' disciples must expect criticism, hostility, and possibly expulsion. But, as Jesus says, "In whose eyes do you want to look good?" Do people give "alms" to Jesus? Does he ever give alms himself? Does he fast on regular fast days (see Mark 14:26)? Does he pray openly in public or in private? Does he model the behavior he demands of his disciples? Is his face and tone of voice different here from what it was in Matt 5:21–26?

Contemplation 12: "And Who Is My Neighbor?" (Luke 10:29–37)

Yes, this is a parable. But it appears as a specific answer to a pointed question, so we take it as a "riposte," even if it serves as an exhortation. Jesus spoke true parable, which Luke and later editors turned into exhortations. "The hands are the hands of Esau, but the voice is the voice of Jacob." He has just taught an aggressive "lawyer" that the apex of the Law is love of God and love of neighbor. But this person "stood up to test Jesus." Typically the attack comes in the form of a question. "Who is my neighbor?" Usually Jesus answers hostile questions with his own question, as he eventually does at the end of his discourse: "Which of these three was a neighbor to the man who fell victim to the robbers?" (10:36). In this case, the very story itself is the answer, without the moral coda; moreover, Jesus lets the man answer this own question, which in the venacular is called "hoisted on your own *petard*." So much for the narrative structure.

It helps to imagine that Jesus' peasant audience would have strong feelings about the characters and events in the story, unknown to a modern listener. For example, robbers were ubiquitous, so the victim was a fool to go alone on a dangerous way—no sympathy here, rather smirks and smiles. The man is a fool. But the "priest" and "Levite" who pass by the victim likewise get the audience's scorn, for their "purity concerns" trump common expectation of help for victims. Their roles and statuses in one sense offend peasants, who know them as the elites who demand a tithe on all that peasants produce, just for their being priests and Levites. Tithes, of course, never benefit those taxed.

Along comes the most unlikely person to give aid: a Samaritan. He is not even an Israelite, but an apostate, and a merchant to boot. He is held in contempt by peasants because in a "high context" environment they all know: "merchants buy cheap and sell dear." That is, merchants live only and always at the expense of the buyer; merchants, then, are thieves. This merchant has an animal carrying "wine and oil," traditional trade goods, which he buys cheap and sells dear. But, to the audience's shock, the merchant stops, pours some of his wares on the victim's wounds, sits him on his own animal, and takes him to lodging—all *without cost or even thought of recompense*. And they are not even kinsmen. Finally, this foolish merchant gives the innkeeper what we call a "blank check," a promise to make good on his return all extra expenses for the victim. Barter is the norm with peasants: one gives and one gets, which is also the norm for settling disputes ("an eye for an eye"). But this Samaritan, presumably a "thief" in peasants' eyes, gives outright and seeks no barter or exchange in return (but remember Zacchaeus in Luke 19:2–8). How exceptionally rare this is in peasant's eyes where everything is scarce, and everything proffered is considered a loan to be repaid. How exceptionally foolish! "Lending" was so unusual that Jesus had to command it: "Lend to those in need" (Luke 6:34). But giving without prospect of return is crazy, dumb, and foolish.

What's wrong with this picture? Everything! Ethnic comrades might be expected to aid one of their own, but they don't. An outsider, considered an apostate and a thief, acts foolishly to "give and not get." The norm is no longer "give and get," but "give without expectation of return." If "charity begins at home," this merchant is all the more a fool to be laughed at. But Jesus' takes stock of the shock to his audience and stumps his questioner. "'Who was neighbor to the man in need?' 'The one who showed him mercy'" (Luke 10:36–37). Even the nasty lawyer can figure this one out. Soon we will hear Jesus say, "I came not to be served but to serve," and, "Come, blessed of my Father . . . you fed the hungry and clothed the naked." Imagine Jesus telling this simply as a story, without its function as a riposte. Sound familiar? Imagine the gestures, the body language and the speech which mimics the characters. Imagine the progressive laugh by the disciples at the absurdity of the story. Imagine their faces when an "outsider" becomes an "insider."

Cameo 7: What's with All the Questions?

In Mark alone people ask Jesus questions twenty-four times. None request information, because as all know, people ask questions to trap someone, test him, discredit him, embarrass him, and destroy him. Put simply, people in a "high context" environment know that questions are weapons attacking the person questioned. This is clear in the Gospels where the questioners are often introduced by "To trap him in what he said . . ." (Mark 12:13) or "To test him . . ." (Matt 16:1; Luke 10:25). No one is surprised that "They watched him and sent spies who pretended to be honest, in order to trap him by what he said" (Luke 20:20). Aggressive questions usually begin with "Why do you . . . ?" "Why do your disciples do . . . ?" "By what authority do you do . . . ?" Jesus, however, regularly answers a question with a question. For example, "I will ask you a question; answer me, and I will tell you by what authority I do these things. Was the baptism of John from heaven or from men?" (Mark 11:29–30; see Mark 2:23–26). Since questions are weapons, Jesus fights back with the same stuff.

Public speakers learned how to ask such questions. Quintilian notes: "What is more common than to ask and enquire? Both terms are used indifferently, although the one seems to imply a desire for knowledge, *and the other a desire to prove something*" (*Inst. Orat.* 9.2.6). Questions are asked "not to get information, but to emphasize *our point.*" Some questions "put an audience on the spot, some are calculated to stump an opponent, some to throw odium on the person addressed, and some only to embarrass the opponent." Quintilian, then, illustrates the popular use of questions as aggressive weapons. This is what "questions" are all about.

4

Shaming an Innocent Man to Death

The endeavor of the contemplations of the *Second Week* was to "see more closely" what was happening to Jesus according to the "high context" of his own culture. The goal here is the same, but with the warning that what we see may not be what is really going on. The difference between the way we see in the *"Second Week"* (acute realism for that cultural world) and the way we must see things in the *Third Week* may be summed up by the topic statement that begins *Jesus Begins His "Way" to Jerusalem.* He tells the disciples of the shaming that is characteristic of the terrible fate of prophets.

> Then he began to teach them that the Son of Man must undergo great suffering, and be rejected by the elders, the chief priests, and the scribes, and be killed, and after three days be raised. (Mark 8:31)

Obviously this displeases the disciples, for which Simon Peter "rebukes" Jesus. But when Jesus in turn "rebukes" him, Jesus speaks to all of his disciples, present and future: "You see things as men see things, but not as God sees them" (Mark 8:32). So, how does God see the coming shaming of Jesus, the prophet?

We pick up the story after the Passover Supper, when Judas and the police had already grabbed Jesus. His enemies think that they are winning: they have arrested Jesus, brought him to trial before the Sanhedrin, who *mock* him *and dishonor* him, and who in turn bring him to Pilate, who also *mocks* him at the hands of the soldiers, who *shame* him, and who finally *humiliate* him by taking his life brutally. According to Mark 8:32, God sees that what Jesus' enemies intend to do is not the whole story, for "Ought not the Christ suffer and so enter into his glory?" Pressing the point, there is an alchemy needed by disciples to see the brutality in the narrative but at the same time to see the irony that what the enemies are doing is actually *honoring* Jesus. Last is first; least in greatest.

Our modern default in meditating on the Passion Narrative has been to focus on the wounds of Jesus, to imagine how much they hurt, what obscene amount of pain he suffered, and how his life was taken away by torture and crucifixion. Indeed, all these thing are rooted in the narrative, but the cultural question is, did the disciples and the evangelists focus on them or did they attend to something else? Just what sort of glasses do the followers of Jesus wear when they "see" the narrative in its own culture? Peter's rebuke of the theater of shame to be inflicted on Jesus was wrong, because he did not see things as God does. But to see things as God does is a new viewpoint, new for those whose aim is to imagine Jesus as he undergoes what we have all come to call "The Passion Narrative." Irony is needed. God's point of view versus that of Peter.

Let the alchemy of irony be our correct starting point. Alchemy simply means that something base and crude is transformed into something valuable and noble. So, too, there is an alchemy for culturally imagining the Passion Narrative. The shame that Jesus endures in every scene of the Passion Narrative is ironically at the same time the honoring of Jesus. The enemies perpetrate actions of contempt and disdain, which actions in God's calculus are the very events that in truth become the honoring of Jesus. Jesus himself spoke about this alchemy in diverse ways: weak is strong; poor is rich; last is first; dead is alive (recall Luke 24:26). Paul repeated this in his remark that "The foolishness of God is wiser than the wisdom of men and the weakness of God is stronger than the strength of men" (1 Cor 1:19). The author of Hebrews said it most crisply, "He (Jesus) despised the shame of the Cross" (12:2). So, our task is to learn to see that *shame in men's eyes is honor in God's eyes*; what they revile and mock, God honors and vindicates. Let those who have eyes to see, see beyond the immediate facts.

The imaginative scenarios of the *"Second Week"* all occur in daylight and in open space; they are drawn on a large canvas with the smell of success in the air. Jesus is a "winner!" There is no limit to his power and wisdom. But with his entry into Jerusalem the canvas shrinks. Most of the events in his Passion Narrative occur at night or indoors. The peasant *dramatis personae* of the village are replaced by powerfully armed soldiers and smirking elites. No kindness here! No quarter is given! Jesus enters into a world of shame, as his opponents view things.

This is what the narrative literally tells us. But Jesus has taught us that there are two different sets of glasses with which to imagine these events: those of his enemies and those of his Father. They see very different things and they evaluate them as deadly humiliations, but his Patron and Father sees them as the way to his becoming honorable and glorious, his way to session at God's right hand. Even the disciples hear only shame and mockery at the hands of the elite of Jerusalem, which in their ears means the utter and lasting "shame" of Jesus.

But through another set of glasses, Jesus sees the events as honorable, for they occur according to the plan and purpose of God ("the Son of Man *must*" = God's wise will; Acts 2:23). Moreover, after men shame and mock him, God will *vindicate* and *honor* him ("be raised"). But his disciples hear only the mocking part. "Peter took him aside and began to rebuke him . . . but he rebuked Peter and said, 'Get behind me, Satan! For you do not think the thoughts of God but of man'" (Mark 8:32).

Imagine Peter "rebuking" Jesus to prevent his "Way" to Jerusalem. No wonder Jesus called him a *skandalon*, that is, a rock blocking his way. Jesus, in turn, "rebukes" him and explains what God sees here. God's thoughts are opposed to Peter's thoughts; God's sense of "honor" bleaches Peter's sense of "shame."

It is with this instruction in mind that we being constructing imaginative scenarios about Jesus from his capture to his tomb. This requires that we come to the task with a sense of alchemy and irony. The antagonists act out of hatred and envy to crush Jesus, but ironically what they are doing is actually honoring him. We will see this if we put on the glasses of God. Above all, remember what was said about Jesus in the Letter to the Hebrews: "he endured the cross, despising its shame, and has taken his seat at the right hand of God" (12:2).

Contemplation 1: Watching Jesus Pray (Mark 14:32–42)

We can feel the heaviness of the failed feast as Jesus looks into the sad, frail faces of his remaining disciples: "You will all desert me; for it is written, 'I will strike the shepherd, and the sheep will be scattered'" (14:27). Always hard of hearing, Peter shouts out loyalty, only to be silenced by Jesus (recall 8:31–33). They climb a hill in the darkness and enter an orchard called

Gethsemane, of which it is noted that "Jesus often met there with his disciples" (John 18:2). After Jesus sheds one group of disciples, he selects Peter, James and John to be companions with him in a dreadful experience, which he prefaces with "I am deeply grieved, even to death" (14:34, words taken from Pss 42:5 and 43:5, which is itself a prayer). Then he steps away from them to be absolutely alone. "Alone" is the operative word: the select three sleep, but Jesus is alone with God. He signals his humbleness before God by throwing himself flat on the ground. Words follow, which the sleeping disciples do not hear.

Mark puts on Jesus' lips the words of the prayer Jesus taught them: "Abba, Father, for you all things are possible; remove this cup from me; yet, not what I want, but what you want" (Mark 14:36, words repeated in Matt 26:39 and John18:11). While not the whole prayer, they are the appropriate part of the prayer for this time in Jesus' life. Looking more closely, what does Mark want us to see beside the fact that Jesus prayed? What does this sound like? Silent words, whispered words; is his face downward or upward? Look at his eyes. We see Jesus once again portrayed as a model and teacher of how to pray in general and how to pray this very particular prayer. He prays this prayer, moreover, *three* times, as he models for them the virtue of perseverance in prayer, which he taught regularly to his disciples. The repetition is not because he did not get it right the first time, but because he exemplifies his own exhortation to perseverance in prayer (Luke 11:5–8; 18:2–5). Here Jesus prays the two common forms of prayer: first, he *petitions* God to "remove this cup from me," but balances it with a declaration of *honor and respect*, "not what I want, but what you want." His persevering loyalty to God contrasts with the failure of the sleeping Peter, James and John, who could not persevere, to "watch one hour" (remember, they drank four cups of wine at Supper, while Jesus fasted). His face eventually becomes serene, not sad; he swells with confidence, not fear. He voluntarily accepts his fate, a mark of courage and nobility. His aloneness will shortly be complete when all the disciples flee and leave him alone. See him stand, walk over to the sleeping three and rouse them. See all four of them go out to meet the soldiers. It is night and all is dark and in shadows.

Contemplation 2: Let Me never Be Put to Shame (Mark 14:43–50)

Throughout his career, all challenges which attack Jesus were repelled. Here, however, Jesus changes his strategy and *voluntarily* accepts the shame of a kiss, his capture, and then abandonment. Judas leads some temple police in the dark to an orchard, to which he knew Jesus would come. Money, we are told, drives him. Judas shames Jesus by kissing him—ordinarily a mark of respect—and by addressing him as "Teacher," another mark of respect. What once were marks of honor have sarcastically become mockery. The kiss singles Jesus out so the police can seize him and bind him—another shameful experience. Loss of power and autonomy would be shameful if imposed by someone, but not so if *voluntarily accepted*. This is verified in Jesus' word: "Nobody takes my life from me, but I lay it down of my own accord" (John 10:18). He might have fled to save his life, as the disciples will shortly do, but he said earlier: "Get up, let us be going. See, my betrayer is at hand" (Mark 14:42).

A disciple draws a sword, itself a rebellion that cancels Jesus' teaching to "turn the other cheek" (Matt 5:39). What in the world is a disciple doing with a sword, a weapon belonging only to soldiers and police? Jesus rejects this violent revenge, and himself mocks his captors: "Have you come out . . . to arrest me as a bandit? Daily I was in your temple teaching, and you did not arrest me" (Mark 14:48–49). His honorable public actions trump their night-time shameful behavior. But again, Jesus' surrender is voluntary, because he accepts what follows as God's will, "But let the scriptures be fulfilled." A final humiliation occurs when "All of them deserted him and fled" (14:50). The scene, moreover, models for the disciples the behavior Jesus mandated when they themselves would endure the same thing. But before their experience, Jesus models and dramatizes his "Way" (Mark 13:9–11; Matt 10:17–18). They, too, will be unjustly seized, publicly humiliated, rendered powerless, and put in chains and in prison. "Bless, and do not curse" (Luke 6:28). Keep your eyes on the face of Jesus. See his posture. With what voice does he speak? We all know how humiliated people are when arrested, taken into custody and processed as perpetrators. Is Jesus experiencing similar feelings? Can you tell from his face what he is thinking? Things are very different if the person arrested voluntarily accepts his fate.

Cameo 8: A Noble Death

The funeral orations delivered annually on the anniversary of the death of Athens's fallen soldiers regularly contain these points: *A death is noble if:* 1. it *benefitted* others; 2. it was either *voluntarily* accepted or chosen; 3. the deceased died *unvanquished* in death or not as a victim; 4. the manner of death manifested *virtue*: courage and justice; 5. there was something *unique* about this soldier's death; 6. this death produced *posthumous honors*, such as funeral games, a monument, and annual remembrance; 7. the fallen enjoy a type of *immortality* in the endless praise and glory by the polis; and 8. a *comparison* of "noble" with "ignoble." All of the evangelists know this code, although only John explicitly illustrates each of these items in his portrayal of "The *Noble Shepherd*" (John 10:10–19). What do alchemical eyes see? All of Jesus' actions here are *voluntary*: Jesus goes out to meet the mob; he allows Judas to mock him with kiss and salutation. He declares that it is out of "justice" that he goes, since "justice" means to pay one's dues to those to whom one is obligated (God, family, and polis). His "justice" is found both in his prayer, "Not my will but yours be done," and in his admission, "Let the scriptures be fulfilled" (Mark 14:49). More illustrations of his "noble" death will follow.

Contemplation 3: Let the Games Begins (Mark 14:53–65)

Israel's elite await his capture: "They took Jesus to the high priest; and all the chief priests, the elders, and the scribes were assembled" (14:53), a hostile group already determined to crush Jesus. The place is a spacious, well-lit hall, large enough to hold 50 or so people. All the luxury we can imagine there is funded by the tithes and temple taxes of peasants. When we know how a typical "trial" worked then, we can follow Mark's narrative, identify its parts and appreciate the injustices to Jesus:

Cameo 9: The Parts of a Typical Trial

Arrest: "Have you come out . . . to arrest me as a bandit?" (Mark 14:48)

Charge: Implied now, but stated later: "You have heard his blasphemy!" (Mark 14:64)

False Testimony: "We heard him say, 'I will destroy this temple made with hands, and in three days I will build another not made with human hands.'" (Mark 14:58)

True testimony: "'Are you the Messiah, the Son of the Blessed One?' Jesus said, 'I am; and you will see the Son of Man seated at the right hand of the Power, and coming with the clouds of heaven.'" (Mark 14:62)

True testimony rejected: The high priest said, "Why do we still need witnesses?" (Mark 14:62–63)

Verdict: "'What is your decision?' All of them condemned him as deserving death." (Mark 14:64)

Sentence: Pilate went out to them, "What accusation do you bring against this man? . . . They replied, "We are not permitted to put anyone to death." This was to fulfill what Jesus had said indicating . . . the kind of death he was to die." (John 18:29–32).

The most important part of an ancient trial was the testimony of witnesses pro and con. In an honor-oriented world, the testimony of a high-ranking, honorable person trumped all other witnesses (see the honorable witnesses whom Jesus calls in his trial in John 5:33–46). If we keep looking at Jesus as teacher and model, we note that he is *silent* in the face of false witnesses, a kind of honorable behavior whereby he refuses to recognize silly challenges to himself. He refuses to play the game. Is this *turning the other cheek?* His studied *silence* provokes the high priest to challenge Jesus directly: "The high priest asked Jesus, 'Have you no answer? What is it that they testify against you?'" (14:60). Questions, which are always challenges, are rebuffed once more, but now with *silence*: "But he was *silent and did not answer*" (14:61). He simply refuses to play the game. The high priest attacks Jesus with another question, which is an open trap for him: "Are you the Messiah, the Son of the Blessed One?" Now Jesus speaks, not to defend himself but because he pledged himself earlier to honor the will and plan of God ("Abba, Father, . . . not what I want, but what you want," Mark 14:36). So, he speaks now, to honor his Patron and Father.

Imagine an elite figure, expensively well dressed and groomed, presumably seated, shouting at a lowly figure in peasant's clothes, whose arms are bound and who is forced to stand. Their speech is also contrasting. Jesus speaks because of the priest's question and his answer is the core of his gospel. What tone does he take here? He publicly honors his God who will shortly honor him: "'You will see the Son of Man seated at the right hand of the Power,' and 'coming with the clouds of heaven'" (14:62). Smug? Confident? Courageous? Disciples later remember how Jesus thrice foresaw his mockery and death, but *also his vindication*: "He began to teach them that the Son of Man must undergo great suffering . . . and be killed, and *after three days be raised*" (8:31). "Raised" here means "seated at God's right hand," the most honorable place in the cosmos. Is he repeating the faith in God he professed earlier? Is this new for him?

But his testimony is shouted down. His judges consider what he said to be impossibly false; Jesus to them is a fool, who shamefully claims the favor of their high Patron. Once again, what is shameful in men's eyes is honorable in God's eyes—silence to false accusations; but speech to affirm God's honor. "Son of Man" refers in the Scriptures to holy people shamed on earth but honored by God in heaven. So, Jesus' remarks speak to his "justice," that is, his faithfulness to God's plan and purpose, even as he "suffers and so enters into his glory" (Luke 24:26). Again imagine how contrasting is the speech and the delivery of the two characters here. "Blasphemy," they shout. "Blasphemy!" God could never vindicate a fool such as this! As the judges condemn him to death, where is justice? An innocent man is condemned. Mockery and shame have their day: they spit on him (surely in his face), blindfold him, and to strike him (again, in the face), saying to him, "Prophesy!" One's face and head are the most honorable parts of the body, which are generally treated with respect (we kiss faces, anoint heads), but now they are the stage of mockery and humiliation. Imagine the face, voice and gestures of Caiaphas. Then look carefully at Jesus' face, both when he is silent and when he speaks. Is he shamed by any of this? Is Jesus continuing to model behavior for the disciples, who will face the same crises (see Mark 13:9–10).

Contemplation 4: Release the Guilty and Condemn the Innocent (Mark 15:1–15)

Jesus' enemies bring him to the Roman governor for execution. In that "high context" world, Israelites stoned blasphemers, but only Romans publicly crucified criminals. Since Pilate's interest is only about Rome's affairs, he asks: "Are you a king, a rival of Caesar?" (Mark 15:2). He dismisses Jesus' response as innocuous, and so renders a verdict of innocence. The trial should be over. When his attackers accuse him of many things, he again is honorably *silent*, for he cannot be challenged by their trivia. A commanding figure in a toga is seated before elders, who are standing and shouting for blood. A common comparison is drawn: Jesus, presumably innocent, is juxtaposed to Barabbas, a genuine rebel and murderer. No "justice" here: his attackers would acquit the guilty and condemn the innocent, compounding Jesus' hurt and mockery: "Release Barrabas and crucify Jesus!" Pilate perceives that it is "out of envy" that the elites hand Jesus over, attesting to the success of Jesus and their failure. And he declares Jesus innocent a second time, "What evil has he done?" (Mark 15:14). How curious for a judge to ask such a question, but not make a declaration of innocence. His "What evil?" is smothered by their "Crucify him!"

The Pilate of history was never this weak; on the contrary, he was renowned for his heavy-handed provocations of Israel, which led to his removal from office. But the Roman judge here lets the genuine rebel and murderer go free, and so becomes complicit in condemning the innocent to death. If it is claimed later that Jesus was justly condemned and executed, the hearers know better (see the rumor about his "empty tomb," Matt 28:11–15). Jesus' treatment by his captors thus far has been remarkably free of physical abuse. But the clouds of mockery begin to rain down over him.

Suggested elements of a "noble death" here include: 1. Jesus' "justice" to God, but pervasive injustice to Jesus (evil is acquitted, but innocence is condemned); 2. comparison of healer with murderer; 3. the "odds" are honorable: a single peasant confounding an entire Sanhedrin and a Roman procurator; and 4. the nobility of "silence," which is louder than "shouting." Do you recognize any "nobility" in Jesus here? What does it look like?

Contemplation 5: Shame Hurts Worse than Pain (Mark 15:16–20)

When Bayer aspirin appeared in 1892, it banished pain. Such an analgesic was unavailable to Jesus and his world. Everybody experienced pain, and little was said about it. Only once is a person's pain noted (Matt 4:24). In Jesus' cultural world, however, what hurts worse than pain is mockery, ridicule, and humiliation, which is the dynamic of this scene. We note that all evangelists basically skip over the details of Jesus' flogging, for although they mention it, they do not report it by a main verb, but in the lesser, participial form, "having flogged him." No details are given, suggesting that the disciples focus on what befalls Jesus next, his mocking. The soldiers stage a mock coronation of a vainglorious "king," which disciples will imagine as ironic events. Was he not the King of the Jews?

Cameo 10: Two Types of Flogging

Type one, a severe beating to one condemned to death to weaken him, shame him, and hasten death (Mark 15:17; Matt 27:26); and type two, the public shaming of a "troublemaker," beaten in the public agora to heap shame on him, prior to expelling him from the city (i.e., "run him out of town"). "I will discipline him and release him" (Luke 23:16, 22). Paul reports that he regularly received the second type of flogging: "with countless floggings . . . five times I have received from the Jews *forty lashes minus one.* Three times I was *beaten [by Romans] with rods*" (2 Cor 11:23–25). Romans beat with rods, but Israelites with belts. All beatings preceded Paul's being expelled from a city. Jesus received the first type of flogging, which was mentioned, but only in passing: "Jesus, *having been flogged,* Pilate handed him over to the soldiers" (Matt 27:26); "Jesus, *having been scourged,* Pilate delivered him" (Mark 15:17).

Note how often Jesus is stripped naked and re-clothed—three times. If a man voluntarily disrobes, he is not shamed, but if his clothes are pulled off him and others strip him naked, he experiences shame. Off come his tunic for flogging, on goes a cloak of bright color, some tint of "purple," a *royal color.* He is *enthroned* on a stool, and soldiers weave a *crown of "acanthus"* ("acanthus" is the Greek word for the vegetable used for this wreath; think "thistle"); a *rod of power,* a reed, rests in his hand. The soldiers then mockingly stage the *coronation* of this false king: "They saluted him, '*Hail, King* of the Jews!' . . . struck his head with a reed, spat upon him, and knelt down in homage to him" (15:18–20). Mark's focus is not on the physical pain Jesus suffers here, which in this case is moderate, but on the mocking insults Jesus endures [strike his head . . . spit on him . . . knelt in homage]. Mark summarizes this by the culturally significant remark: "*After mocking him . . .*" (15:20). How frequently does this experience of Jesus exemplify the fate of true disciples: "How honorable are you when people revile you and persecute you and utter all kinds of evil against you falsely on my account" (Matt 5:11); "Whoever wants to be first must be last of all and servant of all" (Mark 9:35). When disciples remember Jesus' words, they will know how God reverses such mockery and humiliation: "All who are humiliated will be exalted" (Matt 23:12; Luke 14:11; 18:14). Of course, Jesus was *silent* through all this mockery. Do you see any alchemy here; what does Jesus look like when they humiliate him. Is this all loss for Jesus? Is there another way he (and we) might view what is happening? Remember, he himself will say later that the Christ enters into his glory by suffering shame.

Contemplation 6: "He Despised the Shame of the Cross" (Heb 12:1–2)

Again, the evangelists tersely note that he was crucified by narrating it only by a participle, "after being crucified . . ."—a telescoped mention of an event, which is not described.

Cameo 11: *Everyone Knew What Crucifixion Looked Like*

The evangelist operate in a "high context" world, which presumes that all know about crucifixion. They know that the "cross" is only a *cross bar, (i.e. the horizontal piece of wood)*, as long as a man's outstretched arms, which the person to be executed himself carried. The vertical *upright* was already planted in the ground atop which "crosses" were fastened. The upright with body would measure less than 6' from top to ground—easily assailable by passers-by. Bodies were fixed to "the cross" with ropes, nails, or both. Jesus was nailed through his wrists; his legs were bent so that each ankle flanked a side of the upright and his legs were bent and the heel of each foot was nailed to the upright. All these holes in the wood were already drilled, just awaiting another body. The body's entire weight hung from the arms, until they cramped, and the body sagged, and breath could not be breathed. So he pushed up with his legs to allow him to breath. Inevitably, the legs also cramped and the arms again took the whole weight. This progressed to the point that the crucified person could no long pull up or push up because of cramping arms and legs; he asphyxiated slowly, expiring with a whisper. To speed up this process, the executioners regularly broke the legs, so the crucified could not push up for breath (John 18:31–32). He was crucified naked.

Few actual events of the above scene are narrated. Scant attention, moreover, is give to pain, for the story focuses entirely on *shame*. The executioners stripped Jesus naked once more, then, "They divided his clothes among them, casting lots to decide what each should take" (15:24). Naked once more! One more humiliation! The narrative center of this tableau describes three groups of mockers who pass by Jesus and taunt him. This mockery is all that the evangelist has to say about the event; noting else is narrated. But it is bitter indeed.

> Those who passed by *derided* him, *shaking their heads* and say-
> ing, "*Aha!* You who would destroy the temple and build it in three
> days, save yourself, and come down from the cross!" (15:29–30)

We can hear the sarcastic tone of voice, the sense of triumph in the shouting. Those mocking Jesus are probably elites, because the remark about "the
temple" repeats the accusation against Jesus earlier before the Sanhedrin
(14:58). Their mockery centers about the ironic command to "save yourself." His name, "Jesus," means "He will save his people" (Matt 1:21); these
taunters surely know of his prolific "saving" of sick people. But whatever
power Jesus had has now evaporated; now he himself needs "saving." Yet,
Jesus has many times declared that this is the will of his Father, who will
vindicate him. Only in God is there true "salvation" from death. To his tor-
mentors, however, this is just a turn on the wheel of fortune for a fool.

A second group of mockers play the same game with Jesus: they address him with sarcasm to come down, and claim that they will then become disciples. Again, Jesus is silent.

> *In the same way* the chief priests, along with the scribes, were
> also *mocking* him among themselves and saying, "He saved oth-
> ers; he cannot save himself. Let the Messiah, the King of Israel,
> come down from the cross now, so that we may see and believe."
> (15:31–32)

The acid in their mockery repeats the sarcastic remarks about "saving others," but now also his own impotence to "save himself." In their eyes, Jesus'
shame is proportionate to his loss of power, and now Jesus has no power
whatsoever. New insults occur when this group mocks his Israelite preten-
tions to be its Messiah and King—clearly foolish and vainglorious claims
which end in disaster. And Jesus was silent. Shame, however, hurts more
than pain.

Finally a third group of mockers appear: "Those who were crucified
with him also *taunted* him" (Mark 15:32). Although Mark does not record
the content of their mockery, Matthew does: "The bandits who were crucified with him also taunted him *in the same way*" (Matt 27:44). In time disciples would recall the mockery described by Jesus on his "Way" (10:33–34),
understanding how their following of him must include "deny yourself and
take up your cross" (8:34). This remark, we know, spoke not to physical suffering but to sharing in his humiliation and mockery. If they see him more
clearly, they must follow him more nearly and share in his shame. Since you
imagine that you are present, what have you to say to Jesus?

As regards a noble death, 1. Jesus is *silent* throughout, the virtue of self-control; 2. by this he *defeats* those who mock and heckle him; 3. when we view all this with irony, the perpetual mocking that "Jesus saves others" is actually true; he has always been *benefitting* others, even by his death. Yes, it was ironically a "noble death." To unbelieving eyes, Jesus is totally defeated, but not in the eyes of his disciples, at least not yet. He will shortly declare the irony of "suffer many things" to enter the kingdom of God. Even here, do you see in your heart any alchemy?

Contemplation 7: Jesus' Dying Words; What Did He Say? (Mark 15:33–37)

"At three o'clock Jesus cried out with a loud voice, 'Eloi, Eloi, lema sabach-thani?' which means, 'My God, my God, why have you forsaken me?'" The tradition of recording the dying words of someone is ancient, i.e., Caesar to Brutus, "*Et tu, Brute.*" But Jesus' dying words are not a curse or a surrender, because "My God, my God . . ." is a *prayer,* the opening line of Psalm 22. In a "high context" world, disciples could be presumed to remember the whole psalm and recognize these words as *a prayer,* knowing that more than just the first verse of Psalm 22 is intended. After all, several other verses of this psalm have been alluded to in the crucifixion scene:

Psalm 22	Psalm 22 in the Passion Narrative
They *divide my clothes* among them-selves, and for *my clothing* they *cast lots.* (Ps 22:18)	They *divided his clothes* among them, *casting lots* to decide what each should take. (Mark 15:26)
All who see me *mock* me; they make mouths at me, they *shake their heads* (Ps 22:7)	Passers-by *derided* him, *shaking their heads* and saying, "Aha!" (Mark 15:29).
Commit your cause to the LORD; *let him deliver him,* let him rescue the one in whom he delights!" (Ps 22:8)	He *trusts* in God; *let God deliver him now,* if he wants to" (Matt 27:43).
"*My God, my God, why have you forsaken me?*" (Ps 22:1)	"*My God, my God, why have you forsaken me?*" (Mark 15:34)

This correspondence, of course, is studied, not accidental; remember how Jesus said that he would "fulfill the Scriptures." Just as Jesus prayed the "Our Father" in the Garden as an example for his disciples, so now he prays from Israel's prayer book, the Psalms, namely Psalm 22. The bystanders, as always, misunderstand what Jesus says, confusing "Eloi" with "Elijah"—after all, they are outsiders, who do not have "ears to hear." Moreover, even modern disciples do not appreciate that Jesus *prays* a known prayer as his dying words, Psalm 22. Some label it a cry of despair or a failure of faith. Mark intends just the opposite, for he reads Psalm 22 as *a singular testimony of faith*. Those who know the psalm recognize its type as a "complaint" to God, who seems to be slow in responding to the faith of the petitioner (see Pss 10:1; 44:24; 74:1; and 79:10). Pause here to read Psalm 22 as Jesus would have prayed it. Psalm 22 is structured in three parts, each part declaring first the distress of the person praying, which is then balanced with a powerful expression of faith, thus producing antiphonal statements of distress, then faith/loyalty—three times.

| 22:1 *My God, my God, why have you forsaken me?* Why are you so far from helping me, from the words of my groaning? 22:2 O my God, I cry by day, but you do not answer; and by night, but find no rest. | 22:3 Yet you are holy, enthroned on the *praises* of Israel. 22:4 In you our ancestors *trusted*; they *trusted*, and you *delivered* them. 22:5 To you they cried, and *were saved*; in you they *trusted*, and were *not put to shame*. |

The situation is truly wretched, especially because the afflicted person prays constantly but finds no comfort. Yet his faith is indeed strong, especially in the face of fearful terror. As he claims, he comes from *good stock*, "his ancestors *trusted . . . trusted* and were *delivered*; they *cried* and were *saved . . .* they were *not put to shame*." He, then, was raised in a house of faith and he himself is a chip off the old block. He claims the same faith as his ancestors.

| 22:6 But I am a worm, and not human; *scorned* by others, and *despised* by the people. 22:7 All who see me *mock at me; they make mouths at me, they shake their heads*; 22:8 "Commit your cause to the LORD; *let him deliver him—let him rescue the one in whom he delights!*" | 22:9 Yet it was you who *took me from the womb*; you *kept me safe* on my mother's breast. 22:10 On you I was cast from my birth, and since my mother bore me *you have been my God*. 22:11 Do not be far from me, for trouble is near and there is no one to help. |

Not only did his ancestors trust God, but the one praying the psalm claims that he too has been very close to God and has previously known God's favor, from the womb and from his mother's breast. God hallowed his life's beginning: "since my birth, you have been my God." Based on this personal favor, he appeals for God to remain faithful to him: "Do not be far from me, for trouble is near and there is no one to help." He comes from faithful stock, and he is a chip off the old block.

22:12 Many bulls encircle me, strong bulls of Bashan surround me; 22:13 they open wide their mouths at me, like a ravening and roaring lion . . . 22:16 For dogs are all around me . . . My hands and feet have shriveled; 22:17 I can count all my bones.	22:19 But you, O LORD, *do not be far away*! O *my help, come quickly to my aid!* 22:20 *Deliver* my soul from the sword, my life from the power of the dog! 22:21 *Save* me from the mouth of the lion! From the horns of the wild oxen *rescue* me.

These are not complaints as in vv. 1–2, but petitions that are rooted in faith, certainly not despair. His petitions speed to God's throne: *"be not far away . . . come to my aid . . . deliver my soul . . . save me . . . rescue me."* If the bystanders mistook "Eli, Eli . . ." as a cry to Elijah to save him, the disciples will know that Jesus spoke to God as the only, sure source of his salvation. The disciples would certainly *not* see these dying words as a loss of faith, but just the opposite. Thus a person imagining a cultural scenario will study the psalm and imagine how it is woven into the crucifixion scene. Most importantly, this person will try to hear Jesus praying the whole psalm, both the dark parts and their counterbalancing confessions of faith. How, then, does the person imagining the scene view the very dying of Jesus? Is this a time to "have that mind within you which was in Christ Jesus"? (Phil 2:5). What does imitation of Jesus mean now?

Contemplation 8: Finally, Honor, and Respect (Mark 15:38–47)

The charge that Jesus spoke of the destruction of the temple was made before Caiaphas and now when he is on the cross. Still a third repetition of it occurs in Mark's note that "The curtain of the temple was torn in two, from top to bottom" (15:38). Although the temple still stands, we learn that Jesus did not mis-speak, but that his word was validated in an unusual way: the curtain (90' tall, of very heavy fabric) was torn *"from top* to bottom," something no mortals could do, but only God. We consider this, then, as God's own testimony to the correctness of Jesus' words. God vindicates Jesus' word and continues judgment of the old institution (11:15–17). Moreover, if Jesus' Roman judge earlier declared him innocent (15:14), now his Roman executioner likewise changes his mind about Jesus: "When the centurion saw that in this way he breathed his last, he said, 'Truly this man was a son of God'" (15:39). This pagan attests to the innocence of Jesus and to his holiness vis-à-vis God, for "Son of God" means just that, a person close to God and favored by God. Nevertheless it clashes with the mockery hurled at Jesus just hours ago: "Savior . . . Messiah . . . King of Israel." Thus, we finally hear true testimony by an eyewitness to Jesus' holiness—first, God's testimony about the truth of Jesus' word about the temple and then the centurion's testimony about the innocence of man just crucified. Mockery is offset by marvelous things; shame is yielding to honor. Yet Jesus is still dead and needs to be buried. Aren't these events meant to say that God heard the dying prayer of Jesus and validated it?

Contemplation 9: He Is Laid to Rest, Presumably to Remain There (Mark 15:42–46)

As Jesus was dishonored by mocking him, conversely honor and respect attend his burial. Intimates and family members observed his death, especially women with a long history of loyalty to Jesus, who, because of gender conventions, "were looking on from a distance." An ambiguous figure, Joseph of Arimathea, a "respected council member," appears to have been a disciple of Jesus, although in secret for fear of his peers (John 19:38). When Pilate accepted the testimony from the centurion that Jesus was indeed dead, he released the body to Joseph for burial. Sometimes bodies were further dishonored by denying them burial; they might be left on the cross as food for birds and animals—an ultimate form of shame. Not so with Jesus. "Joseph bought a linen cloth, took down the body, wrapped it in the cloth, and laid it in a tomb that had been hewn out of the rock. He then rolled a stone against the door of the tomb" (15:46). More marks of respect. The women saw where the body was laid.

Those imagining this scene should remember that they are at a funeral and burial, albeit one totally unlike one that they themselves might have attended in the past. Remember, the greater your concern for the deceased, the more bitter the burial. How do you feel about Jesus? Where and with whom would you stand? What are your thoughts? Your gestures? Your words? What are you thinking as you eventually leave the place?

Cameo 12: A Stone Cold Tomb

A typical burial consisted of washing the corpse (Acts 9:37), wrapping it in a shroud (Matt 27:59–60), and perfuming it with spices (Luke 24:1). The dead are buried the same day, because corruption started immediately. Outside the tomb all was lamentation and other rituals of distress (Mark 5:38), natural or hired. Because of the strong sense of identity of individuals with their extended family (Matt 8:21), the dead were interred in family tombs, mostly in the ground, but sometimes in shafts cut into the soft limestone, leaving "benches" on each side atop which the corpses were laid (see John 20:12). A round stone (4' diameter, 6"-8" thick) sealed the tomb. Jesus' burial was rushed, so that the typical courtesies, not possible on the death day, would be rendered later.

5

From Tomb to Throne

This part of the gospel begins in sunshine. The horror and sadness of the previous days has melted like fog, and so all postures, facial expressions, tones of voices, and gestures will now reflect victory. The music we sing will be brisk and bright; the horizon will be bathed in pastel colors; and all creatures of our God and King will cry out with gladness. Yet various processes are at work, which begin in the hue of yesterday and only slowly brighten.

Contemplation 1: "We Don't Know Where"
(John 20:1–2, 11–18)

Mary Magdalene finds a way out of the locked city and foolishly goes alone in the dark into dangerous territory, behavior anathema to women who guarded their reputations. The tomb is open and the stone rolled away, hence the obvious question, "Where is his body?" Mary reports this bad news to Peter and the Beloved Disciple that Jesus' body has gone missing, stolen probably, another act of mockery. She speaks a remark that becomes a regular chant for her: "We *do not know where* they have laid him" (Jn 20:2). Two items: first, she is "*not in the know*," and second, she does not know "*where he is*." She returns to the tomb, pokes her head inside, and sees angels, who ask her, "Why are you weeping?" She answers honestly, "They have taken away my Lord, and *I do not know . . . where* they have laid him" (John 20:13). Still "not in the know," she goes outside and mistakes Jesus for a caretaker and says for a third time: "If you have carried him away, *tell me . . . where* you have laid him" (John 20:15).

He answers her in a generous and comforting voice. Her face and posture suddenly look upright, even as she hears her own name, "Mary!" Now her question about *"not knowing"* and *"where"* is answered by Jesus himself: "Go to my brothers and say to them, 'I am ascending to my Father and your Father, to my God and your God'" (John 20:17). Now she *knows,* because Jesus tells her the most significant piece of information in the gospel; no one else knows this, so she is singularly honored. *Where?* Back to where he came from, that is, "ascending to My Father and your Father, to my God and your God." If Mary was stunned to find the tomb empty of its corpse, she is immeasurably thrilled to learn what the empty tomb means, namely, that Jesus survives, goes in honor to the bosom of God, and takes the place he once had. Moreover, being now singularly "in the know" because of Jesus' revelation, Mary is now sent to tell the same good news to the disciples. The messenger of earlier "bad news" now heralds "good news." Her transformation and mission will become the standard for all disciples and apostles: to tell the gospel of Jesus' victory over death. Imagine what she looks like now. If the day began in darkness, it suddenly becomes high noon; if confusing questions clouded Mary's face, now her eyes jump open and her downward frown arches up in a perfect smile. Yes, the vindicated Jesus is important, but the transformation of Mary is also a focal point for those imagining the scene. Imagine everything brightly colored, not just white.

Cameo 13: You Killed Him, God Honored Him

God sent a "beloved son" and empowered him with heavenly Spirit. In turn, Jesus pledged loyalty to God and he died doing the will of his Father. The story of Jesus of Nazareth, however, is not over, for God responds to Jesus. The common way that people spoke of his resurrection was the basic affirmation, "You killed him, *God made him alive.* You mocked him, *God exalted him.* You shamed him, *God honored him."* Hear the gospel of the New Testament.

"Therefore let the entire house of Israel know with certainty that *God has made him both Lord and Messiah,* this Jesus whom you crucified." (Acts 2:36)

"The God of Abraham, the God of Isaac, and the God of Jacob, the God of our ancestors has *glorified his servant Jesus,* whom you handed over to Pilate." (Acts 3:13)

"Let it be known that this man is standing before you in good health by the name of Jesus of Nazareth, whom you crucified, *whom God raised from the dead."* (Acts 4:10)

(Cf. Acts 5:30–32; 10:39–40; 13:28–32; 1 Cor 15:13–15; Eph 1:20; Phil 2:5–11).

Contemplation 2: The Shepherd Searches for His Lost Sheep (Luke 24:13–35)

In late afternoon, two disciples leave the group, intending never to return. While some attribute this to trauma, others observe that they have broken communion with the others, that is, they left the circle forever and do not believe any gospel, certainly not that of the women at the tomb. They will tell Jesus later that they lost their faith, "We had hoped . . ." They are lost sheep, indeed "sinners," for breaking communion and refusing testimony. Their actions are purposeful (they leave) because they have lost faith ("we had hoped"). They leave the city, cross fields, and walk along a dusty path. They quit, as simple as that.

Jesus, however, searches for them. If anyone doubts that Jesus had a sense of humor, his actions now teasingly provoke remarks that an audience would certainly laugh at: "What are you discussing on your way?" As if he does not know! Cleopas interprets Jesus' question as an offensive remark and answers it with his own aggressive question: "Are you the only stranger in Jerusalem who does not know the things that have taken place there in these days?" Jesus' next question is pregnant with irony, rendering it humorous as well. "What things?" Now Cleopas, who disbelieved the gospel told in Jerusalem, repeats the story, but incompletely; his frustration is apparent in his voice and posture:

> The things about Jesus of Nazareth, who was a prophet mighty in deed and word before God and all the people, and how our chief priests and leaders handed him over to be condemned to death and crucified him. But we had hoped that he was the one to redeem Israel. Yes, and besides all this, it is now the third day since these things took place. Moreover, some women of our group astounded us. They were at the tomb early this morning, and when they did not find his body there, they came back and told us that they had indeed seen a vision of angels who said that he was alive. (Luke 24:20–24)

The facts are all there, and they are all true, only narrated in disbelief. As Jesus was for many people, so for these two he was "a prophet mighty in word and deed," an honorable role crushed by a shameful death. How poignant is the bitter remark: "But we had hoped . . ." that Jesus would effect Israel's freedom. Moreover, "some women of our group" brought a message from angels at his tomb that he was alive. This news, unverified, is the true gospel—but not one accepted yet. Although these two know almost all of the pieces of the story, the pivotal one is missing, namely, belief in the testimony by others that Jesus has been raised.

When Jesus calls them "fools" [Greek = *morons*], he certainly gets their attention. The insulting word, however, comes from smiling lips, as he graciously provides the puzzling last pieces. He picks from the Scriptures stories of the holy and wise, who were rejected by their own people, but whom God honored, starting with Abel, Joseph, Moses, Jeremiah, etc. He draws the proper conclusion: "Was it not necessary that the Messiah should suffer these things and then enter into his glory?" (Luke 24:26). Hasn't this been the pattern for holy people all along?

Rejection is overcome with honor! They remark later how these words (imagine tone, pitch, pacing) of this stranger inflamed their hearts, brought them great consolation, and restored the hope they had lost. Again, study the faces, watch them change. Furthermore, we imagine Jesus, still unrecognized, teasing them a third time by saying good-bye and turning on to another path. Their plea is totally sincere: "No! Stay with us! Night falls. Travel is dangerous." After moving away from him in Jerusalem, they cannot now voluntarily let him go. So, they take him home, fetch bread and begin to eat. Usually the host blesses the food, confirming his role and status, but here Jesus takes the bread, blesses it, breaks it, and gives it to them. Now this piece of their Jesus history illumines their minds, "This is Jesus' conventional blessing of food. This is what he always did while alive. This is Jesus!"

What a transformation—from "we had hoped" to "knowing that Jesus is alive," from the ignorance of "Morons!" to proclamation of the full story; from sinners who abandoned the group to believers who return to the group to announce the gospel, which hours ago they found impossible to accept. "They told what had happened on the road, and how he had been made known to them in the breaking of the bread" (24:35). Seeing Jesus more clearly, disciples will surely be reminded of the parable about the foolish shepherd searching for his lost sheep (Luke 15:4–7), now illustrated by Jesus continuing his shepherd's role by seeking out these two lost sheep. Smiles all around! Rushing foot steps! New strength abounding!

Contemplation 3: Shepherd Once More Gathering His Sheep (Luke 24:36–49)

All the disciples are now back together: "The eleven and their companions gathered together, saying, 'The Lord has risen and appeared to Simon!'"

The Emmaus pair add their experience of the risen Jesus. Faces glow, voices are loud, excitement all around. Into this enthusiastic circle walks Jesus, but suddenly their joy becomes fear. "Peace," his signature gesture, does not solve the problem, because some fear that they see a ghost, who comes for retribution for their cowardly behavior. Jesus speaks to the nub of the issue: "Why are you frightened, and why do doubts arise in your hearts?" Why, indeed? But their human hearts demand proof. So, as Jesus showed condescension to the demanding Thomas by displaying his scars, so he extends them to these disciples that they may see more clearly. "'Look at my hands and my feet; see that it is I myself. Touch me and see; for a ghost does not have flesh and bones as you see that I have' . . ." (Luke 24:39–40). Does anyone dare? But they look at them. He wants you to see them and study them. What do you see?

This ought to settle the issue, but their "doubts" stubbornly remain. Again, Jesus offers them proof that he is not a ghost from the realm of the dead, but a live human being in the land of the living. He asks for something to eat, for the simple reason that in a "high context" world all know that ghosts do *not* eat and only those in the land of the living do. We remember Jesus' words to the parents of the little girl whom he brought back to the land of the living: "He directed them to give her something to eat" (Luke 8:55), not because of her exhaustion in dying, but as proof that she was alive, back in the land of the living. We watch him eat, as did the Emmaus disciples, with the same result: "And he took it and ate in their presence." Does Jesus taste anything? Does he chew? Swallow? Does he smile at them? Say anything, such as "Tasty!"

The Risen Rabbi reminds them of all the references about prophets and holy people who were shamed: "These are my words that I spoke to you while I was still with you that everything written about me in the law of Moses, the prophets, and the psalms must be fulfilled" (Luke 24:44). The teacher had said in Emmaus, "'Ought not the Messiah suffer and enter into his glory?' . . . He began with Moses and all the prophets" (Luke 24:26–27), so now he calls to their minds "everything written about him in the law of Moses." He remains their Teacher, their Rabbi. Only now, they see how the Scriptures explain Jesus' rejection and vindication. This scene requires us to use our senses in contemplation: we see violent swings of emotion; we hear joy turn into fear, but back into joy; we examine with the disciples the scars of Jesus and we marvel at him eating. Does anyone touch Jesus?

Contemplation 4: Showing His Scars
(John 20:19–23)

Despite the words of Mary, the situation of the disciples remained acutely fearful. They have locked the doors and sit quietly in the dark "for fear of the Judean elite." To cut off the head of a pernicious group is not enough; the followers must be eradicated to halt this evil once and for all. Police, guards and soldiers are out looking for them, whose voices they hear outside and the shadows of whose torches flicker around them. Suddenly Jesus appears in their midst, an ambiguous figure, who might in their minds be a ghost seeking revenge for betraying and abandoning him. He speaks "Peace" ("harmony in personal relations," itself a word of mercy). But they are still shocked, still fearful, still don't know what to think. He shows them his wounds, not to shame them ("see what you cost me!") and not to prove he is no ghost. We honor service men and women with medals, one of which is the Purple Heart, for being wounded in combat. Best to think of Jesus' wounds as "scars" of battle, demonstrations of his courage. The Greco-Roman world interpreted battle scars as undeniable tokens that one had been cut and bled in the service of the polis or nation, illustrated by the following note:

Cameo 14: Scars in Antiquity = Purple Hearts

Alexander said to his army: "Whoever of you has wounds, let him strip and show them, and I will show mine in turn; for there is no part of my body remaining free from wounds; nor is there any kind of weapon used either for close combat or for hurling at the enemy, the traces of which I do not bear on my person. I have been wounded with the sword, shot with arrows, and struck with missiles, and oftentimes hit with stones and bolts of wood for the sake of your lives, your glory, your wealth." (Arrian, *Anabasis of Alexander* 7.10)

But Jesus has more serious things to do: as Jesus honored Mary with a commission to tell a gospel, so Jesus now dedicates these disciples to continue his own work: "As the Father has sent me, so I send you." This is surely a word of respect for them, cowards though they are. He breathes on them and commissions them: "Receive the Holy Spirit." As Jesus himself "saved his people from their sins," so he continues this though his disciples: "If you forgive the sins of any, they are forgiven them" (John 20:23). This seems a bit odd, because in his Farewell Address, Jesus bestowed on them the legacy of the Holy Spirit, sculpting the work of the Spirit in service to his own gospel, a task of remembering and speaking. Now the Spirit has another function, namely to make present the power of Jesus to forgive and to make holy. How similar this is to Jesus' commission in Luke 24:27, that "Repentance and forgiveness of sins is to be proclaimed in his name." He may vanish, but their eyes have seen him; his wounds were there for the touching, and they were breathed upon by Jesus to continue his work. The former things have passed away; now is a bright new day. Imagine this as another Pentecost. Note also that his Resurrection is not only about himself, but about them and their ministry.

Contemplation 5: Another Lost Sheep Pursued (John 20:24–29)

In the morning, the men did not believe anything the women said about events at the tomb. Now at night, why should Thomas believe this group's proclamation: "We have seen the Lord"? But how would the group think about Thomas? He was strangely absent from the group (as were the Emmaus disciples); he rejected the gospel the others told him (as did the Emmaus disciples). If the Emmaus disciples were "sinners," lost sheep in need of shepherding, so, too, is Thomas. Not "doubting," but very arrogant, proud, and sinful. He demands to inspect Jesus' scars, a shameful challenge to Jesus. His arrogance demands that Jesus march to the beat of his drum. But Jesus returns and says again "Peace be with you"—not just to the disciples, but to Thomas in particular. In an act of immense condescension, Jesus shows Thomas his scars and invites him to complete his demand by touching them (wrists, not hands were pierced; ankles, not feet were nailed; his side, not heart, is envisioned).

We do not know if Thomas actually touched the scars, but Jesus gathers this lost sheep by means of this gracious gesture. Thomas, now given proof of the gospel, believes that Jesus belongs to the heavenly world. Jesus' words to Thomas are intended for the ages and surely belong to later disciples imagining the story of his life: "Have you believed because you have seen me? Blessed are those who have not seen and yet have come to believe" (John 20:29). Visual proof of Jesus' presence is not essential for discipleship, only hearing his voice, "Come, follow me." "Blessed" hardly means happy or joyful; rather, if all value is put in honor and respect, then "How honorable are they who have not seen, but have believed." If Thomas was shamed into believing by physical proofs, "how honorable" are all the rest who follow, not from seeing, but from believing. "Faith," says Paul, "comes from hearing."

Contemplation 6: Chief Fisherman, but So Much More (John 21:1–19)

Don't ask how Peter, who left everything, still has a boat. Rather recall the scene at the beginning of the gospel where Jesus tells Peter to put out to the deep for a catch, despite working all night for nothing. Recall the immense catch of fish, never heard of before in that fished-out lake. Even with help from another boat, Peter and crew are up to their necks with fish, almost sinking. Do you remember hearing Jesus honoring Peter as "Fisher of men"? All these bits of previous stories are intended to be remembered here. Futile labor all night, mysterious instructions to keep working, a net filled with 153 "large" fish. But instead of telling Jesus to "Depart from me, for I am a sinful man," Peter grabs his clothing, jumps in the lake, and speeds toward Jesus. But Jesus now plans to make Peter much more than Chief Fisherman.

On the shore Peter finds a charcoal fire, bread already baked, and some fish grilling on the fire. Who prepared all this? Angels? Mary Magdalene, hiding in the brush? Jesus himself, of course. Once more he feeds his disciples. Remember how bread and fish were twice served to thousands of hungry people. These echoes become a polyphony. But imagine all that Peter sees on the shore, smell it with him, and don't forget to feel the sand. That is why we have senses. Keep remembering that a good shepherd feeds his sheep. As numerous as are the allusions and echoes in this gesture, so are the feelings evoked in the disciples by Jesus' marvelous gesture.

But Chief Fisherman is too little a role for Peter. Balancing Peter's three denials of Jesus in the Passion, Jesus asks three questions about his present loyalty. Recall that Peter "denied" Jesus. "Deny" means, "I do not care what you do to him. He is nothing to me." That denial is erased here by affirmation: "You mean everything to me. I care!" Three denials, three protestations of loyalty. The questions put to Peter also contain a question, "Do you love me more than these?" but this is no challenge. Peter does not take it as such, nor does he answer a question with a question. He responds simply—a new behavior for him. Has he changed? What happened to the rash, boisterous, and prideful Peter? Before, he would boast how noble he was: "Even though all become deserters, I will not" (Mark 14:29). "I will lay down my life for you" (John 13:37). But no longer. He does not compare himself to anyone here, nor does he presume to be wiser or holier than the rest.

The Chief Fisherman is next elevated to the role of Chief Shepherd, a role which belonged originally to Jesus, but which is extended to Peter: "Feed my lambs" (21:15); "Tend my sheep" (21:16) and "Feed my sheep" (21:17). This shepherd's role will truly make Peter follow Jesus and walk in his path.

The "Noble Shepherd" lays down his life for his sheep (10:11). When Jesus told Peter and the rest that he was going where they could not follow, Peter stuck his neck way out: "Lord, where are you going?" Jesus answered, "Where I am going, you cannot follow now; but you will follow afterward." Peter said to him, "Lord, why can I not follow you now? I will lay down my life for you." Jesus answered, "Will you lay down your life for me?" (John 13:36–38). Peter's boast is a claim to be just like the Noble Shepherd, *who lays down his life for the sheep*. Then Peter spoke in pride and arrogance. But now he speaks without arrogance, in tones respectful of Jesus; he has "repented.," that is, he has "changed his mind." Now Peter is ready to be the shepherd who lays down his life. Grace conquers sin once more. And he who was last is invited to become first.

Contemplation 7: A Mountain, a Command, and a Commission (Matt 28:16–20)

Matthew's gospel ends with Jesus joining his disciples in Galilee, as he had said (Matt 28:7). If Jerusalem is a place of mockery and violence, "Galilee" represents a place where Jesus receives respect and honor, even success in finally grooming his disciples. Jesus' address again contains a commission, as did his appearances to Mary Magdalene, the Emmaus disciples, Thomas, and Peter. Now the vindicated Jesus tells us the basis for his command: "All authority in heaven and on earth has been given to me" (Matt 28:18). Prior to this, Jesus confessed that God alone had such sovereignty, a point Matthew wants us to remember: "For mortals it is impossible, but for God all things are possible" (Matt 19:26; cf. Mark 10:27; Luke 18:26). Now, Jesus proclaims that he enjoys a new role and status at the right hand of God, which he had earlier alluded to: "From now on you will see the Son of Man seated at the right hand of Power and coming on the clouds of heaven" (Matt 26:64). They killed him, but God exalted him, seated him at his right hand, and made him Lord of Lords and King of Kings. This Jesus now addresses his disciples, and so they give him honor and respect: "When they saw him, they worshiped him" (Matt 28:17). The Greek word "worship" describes a common posture of respect to someone of higher status; it includes a "kiss of his feet, of the hem of his garment, even of the ground on which he stands." The shameful disloyalty displayed by abandoning him ("Then all the disciples deserted him and fled" [Matt 26:56]) is canceled by the honor and respect shown Jesus now. In this context of renewed attachment, Jesus gives them a command to be just like himself, surely a mark of high respect: "Go and make disciples of all nations, baptizing them in the name of the Father and of the Son and of the Holy Spirit, and teaching them to obey everything that I have commanded you" (Matt 28:19).

When we make an imaginative scenario of this, we locate Jesus on a "mountain," one of his favorite places to teach and pray. Do not think of a forest, but rather of small olive and maybe of fruit trees; the ground will not appear well watered, and there will be stones and weeds. Is Jesus in any kind of festal robe? What color is it? Is it fancy in any way? Is he normal size? Groomed? Spiffy? How does his voice here compare with his speech previously? More solid? Commanding? And what does his face look like?

Cameo 15: Resurrection Appearances as Commissionings

"Go and make disciples of all nations . . ." (Matt 28:19)
"You are witnesses of these things . . ." (Luke 24:48)
"As the Father has sent me, so I send you." (John 20:21)
"Feed my lambs . . . tend my sheep . . . feed my sheep" (John 21:15–17)

As important as were the commissions given by the earthly Jesus (Matt 4:19; 9:9; 10:5–13), the command by Him who has "all authority" is far greater. And it is a commission without limits or terminus: "disciples of *all* nations . . . teaching them *all* that I have commanded you." Just as *"all* authority" is given to Jesus, so the disciples will evangelize *"all"* people" and teach them *"all"* he commands; and he will be with them *"all* days" until the end. So much is packed into that one word, *"all."* No mention is made of performing Jesus' healings or works of power, for the emphasis here is on the "gospel," the proclamation of all Jesus' words, sayings, teachings, parables, and sermons. In short, the full revelation of God will be found in Jesus' teaching, the foundation for discipleship. The heavenly Rabbi has spoken. "I am with you," and urges us to recall the meaning of Jesus' name as drawn from Isa 7:14: "They shall name him 'Emmanuel,' which means, 'God is with us'" (Matt 1:23). It has often been said that there is no nostalgia, no hint of a past "golden age" of the life of the earthly Jesus which later disciple feel they have missed. Quite simply, no one thought years later that they were missing anything, for Jesus seated at God's right hand *continues* his care of his sheep. Although they were previously impervious to Jesus' "Way" of rejecting honor, Jesus now honors them by re-selecting and giving them the fullness of his wisdom and power to call others everywhere and for all times to the flock of Jesus, the Supreme Shepherd. No, his ministry has not ended; all that he said and did continues.

6

"Honor Desired, but Rejected"

Ignatius urges people who are praying not only to "see" more closely, but to "listen" very carefully. If seeing Jesus in his own culture continues to be our aim, then we must "listen" with ears attuned to the channel-clear frequency of his culture, namely "honor and shame." This is not a new language for us, because we call mayors and judges, "Your Honor," and we "honor" our veterans on Memorial Day, and "honor" visitors with the Key to the City. But the cultural world of Jesus was thoroughly obsessed with the desire and search for "honor."

Cameo 16: Honor and Shame: The Consuming Passions

Xenophon (430–355 BCE) described the Athenians as passionate for praise: "Athenians excel all others not so much in singing or in stature or in strength, as in *love of honor*, which is the strongest incentive to deeds of honor and renown" (*Mem.* 3.3.13). Seven centuries later, Augustine in his review of the history of Rome, likewise commented on how the Romans were utterly obsessed with the love of praise and renown: "For the glory that the Romans burned to possess, be it noted, is the favorable judgment of men who think well of other men" (*City of God* 5.12). "He (God) granted supremacy to men who for the sake of honor, praise and glory served the country in which they were seeking their own glory, and did not hesitate to prefer her safety to their own. Thus for one vice, that is, *love of praise*, they overcame the love of money and many other vices" (*City of God* 5.13). This assures us that "love of honor" dominated the values of the Greeks long before Xenophon and of the Romans long after Augustine.

It is always helpful for a "native informant," in this case, Aristotle, to tell us what he and his contemporaries meant by "honor."

> *Honor* is the token of a man's being *famous* for doing good . . . Doing good refers either to the preservation of life and the means of life, or to wealth, or to some other of the good things which it is *hard to get either always* or *at that particular place or time* . . . The *constituents of honor* are: sacrifices; commemoration, in verse or prose; privileges; grants of land; front seats at civic celebrations; . state burial; statues; among foreigners, obeisance and giving place; and such presents as are among various bodies of men regarded as marks of honor. For a present is not only a bestowal of a piece of property, but brings *honor*, which is what the *lovers of honor* desire. (*Rhet.* I.1361a.25–1361b.2, italics added)

Simply put, "honor" refers to the respect, regard, admiration, and esteem in which someone is held. In the jargon of this book, "honor" means *looking good in the eyes of others*. In the eyes of these others we learn the native code of honorable acts, according to which all evaluate the behavior of their peers and neighbors according to what all agree is "honorable." Recall that Jesus rebuked Simon Peter for having a *code of honor* that works in the village, but is totally wrong in God's eyes (Mark 8:31–32). By this pivotal statement Jesus admits that, while there is *a native code of honor* that de-values his future in Jerusalem as folly or shame, the more important *code of true honor* is that which looks good in God's eyes. There are the two sets of glasses through which to evaluate human behavior.

How does one get this most valuable commodity? One may inherit it or achieve it. Inherited honor comes from one's family, place of origin, etc. Persons are considered "honorable" based on the excellency of the place where they were born: Paul was born in Tarsus, "an important city" (Acts 21:39); a resident of Israel's capital may boast, "This one was born in Jerusalem" (Ps 78:6). The converse is also true, for "Can anything good come out of Nazareth?" (John 1:46). Moreover, a person may belong to a noble line ("blue bloods," we say): Paul claims honor because he is "Of the people of Israel, of the tribe of 'Benjamin, a Hebrew born of Hebrews" (Phil 3:5) and "A Hebrew . . . Israelite . . . descendant of Abraham" (2 Cor 11:22). This is the purpose of genealogies (Matt 1:1–17; Luke 3:23–38).

In terms of achievement, one might win twenty-four Olympic gold medals, the annual poetry or drama competition, be the first to swim the Hellespont or climb Mount Everest. But on the village level of unexceptional peasants, one generally challenges someone else, wins and so takes his "honor." The following scenarios illustrate first of all, Jesus' honor ascribed by God, and the second one, the honor Jesus achieves in the push-and-shove of village life.

Example 1: Jesus' Ascribed Honor (Mark 9:2–8)

After telling the disciples of his forthcoming shame, Jesus takes the core three disciples up a mountain where he was "metamorphosed." God made him radiant, clothed him in robes of glory, and brought to him the two greatest prophets, Elijah and Moses. These two prophets experienced the shame of rejection, but then vindication by God, and so exemplify Jesus' own advancing falling and rising. Great company! God, moreover, honors Jesus by commanding the disciples to "Listen to him," because Jesus is God's "Beloved Son." We note what is "honorable" here: 1. God's heavenly attention to Jesus (metamorphosis, clothing, company), 2. God's command to listen to Jesus, and 3. God's own declaration of Jesus' importance ("My Beloved Son). An adequate scenario might include a high mountain, from which one can see everything. Jesus changes shape, for that is what "meta-morphosis" means: what do you see before and after? Same Jesus? What is happening to his person, not just his clothes? Can you read this from his face and gestures. What do you think Elijah and Moses were saying to Jesus (Luke thinks he knows, 9:31)? Follow the radical changes in the posture and behavior of the disciples? Imagine Jesus' posture, gestures and facial features. In the end, what does this mean in regard to the disciples' loyalty to Jesus? Why keep this secret?

Example 2: Achieved Honor (Mark 3:1–6)

One Sabbath, the synagogue became an arena where the Pharisees attacked Jesus. They watched him "so that they might accuse him"—which is a voiceless challenge to Jesus. He counter-challenges them by asking a ques-tion—always an aggressive action. Although he knows the Sabbath norms, here in their midst is a human with a great need, the obviousness of which is evident to all."Is it lawful to do good or to do harm on the Sabbath, to save life or to kill?'" They are silent, or, better, "are silenced." We note what is "honorable" here: 1. the success at rebuffing the hostile challenge;

2. proof that Jesus wins is found in the silencing of the enemies; 3. the rule makers are confounded by Jesus' common sense; 4. the conflict becomes more intense and continuous (they must kill him for revenge); and 5. Jesus is honorable enough to redefine Sabbath observance. The healing is his own action, hence acquired honor, as well as an act of God, hence, ascribed honor.

Admittedly, the pursuit of "honor" is the paramount value of Jesus' world, and its intensity can be sharpened when we know two more cultural things. The entire world was perceived of as "agonistic," that is, all families quarrel with each other . . . always the same squabbles, endless squabbles, passed down from generation to generation in endless lawsuits and feuds. This perpetual conflict exists because all saw the world in terms of "zero sum game": everything in the world exists in limited amounts and when a person steps on the public stage, all good stuff is already apportioned. So, if someone gains, others must be losing. This is how a native described it: "People do not find it pleasant to give honor to someone else, for they suppose that they themselves are being deprived of something" (Plutarch, *On Listening to Lectures* 44B). The enemies of Jesus thought just this way: "If we let him go on, everyone will follow him and abandon us" (John 11:48); even Pilate understood "that it was out of envy that they handed Jesus over" (Mark 15:8). Honor and shame are the principle colors of the narrative palette.

Every New Testament author writes from this perspective, first in telling Jesus' story, then that of the disciples, and then of all of the characters moving though the stories. How could anyone ever attempt to understand the words of Jesus in his own culture *without this compass*? However, as fervently as people seek to look good in the eyes of their neighbors, Jesus declares a counter-teaching, namely, rejection of all earthly honor and replacing it with a search to look good only in God's eyes. Thus his audience as well as his disciples find such teachings severe in the extreme, very opaque to understand, and impossible to follow. No, it is not easy for disciples to "hear him more clearly." But try we must.

Cameo 17: "Honor" in the Spiritual Exercises

Ignatius teaches a pivotal point: for mortals there are two competing ways of gaining "honor." All praying the *Exercises* are confronted with a significant choice, to seek the honor of God or to pursue honor in the eyes of others:

> Thus if he inclines to seeking and possessing an office or benefice, not for the honor and glory of God our Lord, nor for the spiritual well-being of souls, but for his own temporal advantage and interests, he ought to excite his feelings to the contrary and ask God our Lord for the contrary, namely, *not to want* such office or benefice, or any other thing, *unless* His Divine Majesty convinces him that the motive for desiring or having one thing or another be *only the service, honor, and glory* of His Divine Majesty. (*Spir. Exer.* #16, italics added)

Ignatius understood that there are two codes of honor, one of which is to "look good in the eyes of another" and a second one which is to "look good in God's eyes." The religious Order which Ignatius founded adopted as its motto: AMDG, that is, *ad majorem Dei gloriam—all for the greater glory of God*. They are "not to want nor seek any other thing except . . . *the greater praise and glory of God our Lord*. (*Spir. Exer.* #189, italics added)

Example 3: "Rejecting Honor in Others' Eyes" (Mark 1:40–45)

Jesus leaves Capernaum and the brilliant success he had there to wander in Galilee. His disciples do not understand why he abandons so favorable a spot. When all love you, you stay and drink it in. Jesus encounters a solitary man standing 100 meters from him, who shouts, "Unclean," the cry of all lepers. Jesus takes several steps toward him, and the leper does likewise, until they are within touching distance. "A leper," we are told, "came to him begging him, and kneeling he said to him, 'If you choose, you can make me clean.'" Jesus responds with a gesture, "He stretched out his hand and touched him," and spoke "I do choose. Be made clean!" (Mark 1:40–41). Here is a typical honor-achieving encounter. Since a village priest (like Zechariah) likely declared the man a "leper," then a village priest must inspect him to check if he is truly clean and give him a "passport" to return to his village and family. If the man does this, Jesus can go his way without hearing a chorus of shouts of honor and respect. Jesus does not want this attention, and so he commands the man *not* to go home and spread the news, but to go to the priest and do what the law requires, which delay will give Jesus time to move on. Although Jesus has earned honor, he rejects it, establishing a strategy which declares that he cares nothing for honor in the eyes of men (cf. Mark 5:20; 7:24, 36; 8:26, 30).

In summary, there are two avenues to acquiring honor: 1. bestowal by family or superiors and 2. achievement by prowess. Moreover, there are two radically different kinds of honor, that bestowed by one's peers or that awarded by God. The first requires one to "look good in the eyes of one's peer" but the second, "to look good in the eyes of God." Jesus eschews the former and prizes only the latter. To know the mind of Jesus, we need to know his take on "honor." So we read on.

Contemplation 1: No Attack! No Revenge! (Matt 5:21–26)

The first section of the Sermon on the Mount contains "Antitheses," that is, contrasts between old traditions and Jesus' new teaching (Matt 5:21–26). The first contrast reads: "You have heard that it was said, 'You shall not murder'; and 'whoever murders shall be liable to judgment.'" In a world of honor and shame, when a man is murdered, he cannot earn more honor, much less defend what he has, for his earning days are over. *Murder, then, is an aggressive attack on a man's honor. As a victim, the murdered man is permanently dishonored.* Since murder-to-gain-honor is proscribed, so too is murder-as-revenge, the old "eye for an eye." If revenge is proscribed, then the protagonist of the first murder is awarded victory and so gains more honor and respect. He came, he fought, he conquered. Yet Jesus deletes both murder and revenge from his calculus of honor. Jesus, moreover, forbids his disciples to perform any aggressive action to gain more honor or to retaliate in any way. They may not play this game, period!

Not only may they not attack to gain respect, but they cannot even be "angry" when they themselves are provoked. Can this be right? Must one forego revenge and restoration of honor? Jesus says, that far from receiving respect from one's peers, "anger," when acted out, is "liable to judgment," that is, public reproach—but before whom? The elders sitting at the village gate who adjudicate disputes? Then in whose eyes? Far from hearing applause for refraining from anger and vengeance, the disciples will hear censure, that is, "Shame on you" for *not* retaliating. "You coward!" Beyond physical actions of retaliation, even verbal insults will be aired in public, and the paramount insult, "You fool," will bring shame upon those who says it. No sticks and stones, no words which wound.

What is wrong with this picture? Everything! Behavior deemed honorable and manly in the eyes of one's peers is shameful in God's eyes. Not only may disciples *not* attack and so gain honor, but they are proscribed *from* seeking revenge. They cannot seek "an eye for an eye." In the eyes of neighbors, the disciples are shameless, un-masculine, and weak; in US terms, wimps.

When you imagine either these general words or envision a scene illustrating it, you must watch the faces, gestures, and postures of the persons in conflict. Hear not only what they say, but its tone and intent. Imagine Jesus looking at you in such a situation. In whose eyes do you want to look good? What do you think about a world of non-honor? No attack! No revenge! No verbal retorts! You can no longer "Act like a man!"

Cameo 18: Revenge is Sweet

An honorable man *must* retaliate, take an eye for an eye, seek revenge, for revenge was a cultural *necessity*. Failure to retaliate will be judged as cowardice, hence "dishonorable." Thus Aristotle on revenge: "A desire for *conspicuous revenge*" (*Rhet.* 2.2.5). "Revenge, then, is the honorable expression of 'anger,' which may be defined as 'an impulse to a *conspicuous revenge* . . . Hence it has been well said about wrath, 'Sweeter it is by far than the honeycomb dripping with sweetness, and spreads though the heart of men'" (*Il.* 18.109). It is also attended by a certain pleasure because the thoughts dwell upon the act of vengeance, and images then called up cause pleasure" (*Rhet.* 2.2.1–9). The Bard wrote: "Revenge is just, revenge is sweet, and mine, Macbeth, shall be complete."

Contemplation 2: "Love Means You Never Have to Say 'Sorry'"

It gets worse. Jesus cites a case where a man is offering a sacrifice in the temple and remembers that a neighbor *has something against him* (i.e., he, the man offering sacrifice, is the aggressor in the conflict). That's right; the man attempting to honor God with a sacrifice has previously offended someone, in public, of course, and shamed him. He must leave the public sacrifice—a strange thing indeed—and go back to that public place and "come to terms" with his accuser. The verb "come to terms" (or "be reconciled with") has nothing to do with a request for forgiveness. There is no phrase in the Bible which means "I'm sorry." They simply do not apologize. Jacob sought to be "reconciled" with Esau by *sending him rich gifts* "to find favor in your sight" (Gen 32:13–21); David sought "reconciliation" with Saul by *sending him hundreds of heads* of his Philistine enemies (1 Sam 29:4). In that "high context" world, everybody knew that it was culturally impossible to apologize or confess fault in public. The only possible action was to offer some form of *material recompense*, an animal, produce, or wealth; this was the way to call off a feud. Now Jesus teaches his disciples to do the impossible, to call off a public fight and to make public restitution. But all would then say, "See, he starts a fight, but cannot finish it." The disciples, we imagine, would say, "I would rather die than do that!" Look at the crowds: no one is happy. Look at Jesus, note his tone, volume and manner of delivery. Recall the last time you had to admit a fault or tell someone that you're sorry—maybe in private, but in public?. If you did it, bet you did it in private, not in front of the office or amid the family. How did you feel? Then how might the man Jesus instructed to be "reconciled" with his enemy feel? Look at Jesus' face when he gives this exhortation. What facial expression? Watch his eyes and his mouth.

Contemplation 3: In Whose Eyes Do You Want to Look Good? (Matt 6:1–18)

We imagine it specifically as illustrating the major theme of Jesus' preaching, "In whose eyes does a disciple want to look good?" The acts of piety described in Matt 6:1–18 were practiced in public, mostly in the synagogue and in the market place; everyone could see what others did and did not do. Of course God was honored, and those who practiced them before their male peers were deemed honorable in the eyes of others, a side benefit of no insignificant value. This public practice of piety for praise in men's eyes is the target of Jesus' remarks. Practice them, not in public, but in private (i.e., at home). To forego looking good in the eyes of one's peers, a disciple is told to separate himself from the arena of honorable behavior and risk being labeled a non-observant person. This reminds us of Jesus' criticism of scribes who promote themselves in various ways: "Beware of the scribes, who like to walk around in long robes, and to be greeted with respect in the marketplaces, and to have the best seats in the synagogues and places of honour at banquets" (Mark 12:38–39). In constructing an appropriate scenario of Jesus' teaching, imagine a market square with many men constantly in motion, reciting prayers, showing hungry faces, looking stern, living the cultural imperative of wanting to look good in others' eyes. But do you see any of Jesus' disciples in that crowd? Can you tell if they are missed? Where are they? What are the others thinking about them?

"Reward" means *praise and honor*, not from men, but from God in heaven. Money or wealth, then, are not the "reward" of which Jesus speaks, but the respect, honor, and praise God bestows on those who eschew earthly honors. "Looking good in God's eyes, not men's" is a refrain throughout Jesus' teachings and characterizes his own behavior. To be sure, a studied rejection of men's honor will itself be taken as arrogance or folly. The code requires men to practice public piety and refusal to do so will be interpreted as contempt for God and treason toward Israel. Jesus' disciples will assuredly receive criticism, hostility, and possibly shunning.

Cameo 19: In Whose Eyes Do You Want to Look Good?

Do not	blow a trumpet as the hypocrites do in the synagogues or on the streets	be as the hypocrites, for they love to stand in the synagogues and on the street corners	look dismal like the hypocrites, they disfigure their faces
look good in others' eyes;	to be given glory by men;	to be seen by them;	so as to appear fasting;
reward: shame	they have lost their *reward*;	they have lost their *reward*;	they have lost their *reward*;
Do	let not your right hand know what your left is doing;	enter your room and shut the door;	anoint your head and wash your face;
look good in God's eyes	your alms will be "*in secret*."	pray to your Father "*in secret*"	so that you may not appear to men to fast, but to your Father "*in secret*."
reward: honor	And your Father who sees "in secret" will *reward* you.	And your Father who sees "in secret" will *reward* you.	And your Father who sees "in secret" will *reward* you.

Imagine each public and each private scenario in turn: who is present? whom are people noticing? what do they expect? Imagine narrow eyes and pursed lips. Is anyone smiling? At peace? Then "go home" and imagine *who* is doing *what*, *where*, and *why*. What social price do disciples pay if they absent themselves from traditional pious actions? Do you like looking like a fool?

Contemplation 4: Loss of Family, Loss of "Wealth," Loss of Honor

On occasion, sayings of Jesus complement each other, which provides clues on how to understand each one of them. Although positioned in the gospel narratives in various places, the sayings below all give teachings by Jesus on a common topic. For example, the original Beatitudes were only 4 in number, which describe the fate of one man expelled from his family because of Jesus, i.e., a divided household. In a similar vein, Jesus speaks boldly about his own dividing of families. This thread is later found in the exhortation to a husband and wife who have been cut loose from the man's family.

Your author imagined a "high context" scenario about a son expelled from his family for allegiance to Jesus, which is proposed as the narrative behind his teaching. A father, let us call him Abraham, takes his son (Isaac) to synagogue every Sabbath, where Jesus occasionally speaks, whose message and demeanor greatly impress Isaac, to the embarrassment of Abraham. Over the space of many Sabbaths, Isaac disregards the wishes of Abraham—thus causing his father to "lose face" before his peers, even after his father sternly warned him of the harm caused to the family because of Isaac's fascination with Jesus (i.e., collapse of betrothal contracts, rupture of mutual-aid agreements with neighbors, etc.). Finally, considering Isaac a "rebellious son" (Deut 21:18–21), Abraham sends Isaac packing, without any baggage or food or farewell. This represents the scenario described in the last "beatitude": "people hate you, and exclude you, revile you, and defame you on account of the Son of Man" (Luke 6:22). Because there is a close interplay between Luke 6:22 and Jesus' other remarks on family, the fate of Isaac the disciple gives substance to the appropriateness of this scenario.

Since we consider that the story line begins with the Lukan Beatitudes Luke 6:20–23), we start there, and then read the collection of sayings in Luke 12:22–34, and finally in Luke 12:49–53. All three blocks of material are concerned with the same crisis of a fractured family, and so we consider them a unit and read them sequentially to get the whole story for our imaginative scenario. These three remarks are an extended teaching by Jesus on the price paid by disciples whose families are cut in two because of loyalty to Jesus and so cut off a "rebellious son." Besides narrating the complete and bitter price paid by certain of Jesus' followers, they all have to do with the collapse of honor in a son/husband in his family and village, when families expel him and cut him loose. This "loss of honor" derives from his immediate loss of "wealth" and his reduction of status to that of the "begging poor" (in Greek, there are two words for "poor": all peasants are *poor*, but in addition there are "begging poor," the term used in Luke 6:20). Let us eavesdrop on them, for they contain some of Jesus' most significant words.

Luke 6:20–23

We have yet to figure out the right translation for the "beatitudes" in Matthew and Luke. Some think of them as "blessed," but what odd favors does God drop on them? No, nobody should call them "blessed." Certainly people so reduced in straits, moreover, are not "happy," another infelicitous rendering. In Greek, the sayings are called "makarisms," ("fortunate persons who are privileged recipients of divine favor")—still ambiguous. But if we hear them in the key of honor and shame, they might accurately be translated as "How honorable are you (when others shame you) . . ."

Scholars agree that Jesus originally spoke only four makarisms, each prefaced with a grant of praise, "How honorable are you . . ." In Luke these four "honor" statements are paired with their opposite, "How shameful are you . . ."

How honorable are you who are poor, for yours is the kingdom of God.	But how shameful are you who are rich, for you have received your consolation
How honorable are you are you who are hungry now, for you will be filled.	How shameful are you who are full now, for you will be hungry.
How honorable are you are you who weep now, for you will laugh.	How shameful are you who are laughing now, for you will mourn and weep.
How honorable are you when people hate you, and when they exclude you, revile you, and defame you on account of the Son of Man. Rejoice on that day and leap for joy, for surely your reward is great in heaven; for that is what their ancestors did to the prophets.	How shameful are you when all speak well of you, for that is what their ancestors did to the false prophets.

The four verbs in the last "makarism" intensely express "shame": hate, exclude, revile, and defame. We imagine, moreover, that these four refer to only one person, not four different people; they are very *specific*, not general misfortunes. We imagine, moreover, that the last statement is the summary of the previous three, in fact, their cause. If a man's son becomes so enamored of Jesus as to cause scandal in the village, this would likely prompt the patriarch to warn his son, threaten him, discipline him, and finally expel him from the household—not for bad behavior, such a murder or theft, but "on account of the Son of Man," that is, because of loyalty to Jesus. If thus expelled from family (and village, too), the disciple will suffer an immediate collapse of fortune. He will not leave with a month's supply of food in a knapsack, but with nothing; he will instantly become "begging poor." He will instantly become "hungry and thirsty," because he took nothing, not even a water flask. Because he was abruptly cut off from his premiere support system, his family, he will experience a "death" of all kinship, and so he will truly mourn his loss of family. No one will aid him, when his own family holds him in such contempt.

Our construction of a scenario of other related saying needs a fuller picture, but at this point, Jesus exhorts would-be disciples to appreciate the cost of lost honor to be paid for being his disciple, just as he does later when he cautions against rash decisions: like going to war without enough troops or starting a tower without adequate materials (Luke 14:25–33). Don't start if you cannot finish it. You will look like a fool.

One might imagine the faces, gestures, and voices of the family who chase away the rebellious son. They all agree with the patriarch. They are all very hurt by the son's behavior. Then imagine the face and feelings of the son sent packing. Note if he takes *nothing* with him from the family house. Imagine his first night exiled from his family security; empty the space around him, for no one will come to his aid. Above all, imagine Jesus speaking this, his delivery, his aim, his concern.

Cameo 20: *Family Benefits*

The typical "family" in Jesus' time was the "household" of the father/patriarch, which was often in the center of a compound of his own sons and his brothers. A typical family probably owns some land, at whose cultivation all members labor and whose fruits all enjoy. A typical family would be very traditional, highly suspect of change or novelty; and so, all are expected to think alike and value the same things. Since "charity begins at home," any economic crisis in one part of the family would activate the rest to come to the aid of those in need. When all is working well, members are housed adequately, fed substantially, clothed sufficiently, and share prosperity. Few indeed are recorded as voluntarily leaving this "family," because survival without it is perilous at best and fatal at worst. Now imagine the person in Luke 6:20–23 who has been expelled from this ancestral house.

Luke 12:22–31

This exhortation, of course, could appear just about anywhere in the gospel narrative. But ancient sources link it to remarks just studied above about a man expelled from his family. This connection suggests that we imagine the expelled son and his wife lamenting their precipitous ill-fate. They are begging poor, mourning and very hungry. We imagine the specific context of these words to be Jesus' balm on their troubled waters. The story unfolds in typical gender-divided perspective. The first half is addressed to the husband, the second to the wife. Both talk about the gender duties of each: the man with agriculture and food production and the female with clothing production.

A general exhortatory word prefaces the story: "Do not worry about your life, what you will eat (male concern), or about your body, what you will wear (female concern)." Why? "Life is more than food, and the body more than clothing." This sounds very generic, until Jesus addresses first the male and then the female, not in generic terms, but in regard to the great losses suffered recently by expulsion from the family. What is *not in view* is land, family land, on which to grow food to eat and pasture animals for wool to weave cloth. In a male space, outdoors, it is easy to imagine lots of birds flitting from trees and bushes: "Consider the ravens: they neither sow nor reap, they have neither storehouse nor barn, and yet God feeds them." Like the birds, the man owns no lands, crops or barns. He is bereft of all of these, but he is consoled to know that he is worth many, many birds in God's eyes. The female, normally within a compound with other females, is outdoors where she can see "the lilies, how they grow." They are more honorable than Solomon in his royal and honorable finery. If lilies fade, dry up quickly and become tomorrow's fuel, a female, wife and maybe a mother, should know how much more valuable (honorable?) she is than mere wild flowers.

Imagine Jesus actually saying these words; imagine his audience, not a generic audience but specific people within the group of his disciples. Imagine his delivery, his intent in saying these words, and what effect he strives to achieve. Does he point to the sky? Bend low to the grass? What facial expressions does he show here? Imagine these words being said to the person who is the protagonist of 6:20–23. Why does Jesus say them? What purpose has he?

Luke 12:49–53; Matt 10:34–39

Here Jesus makes it clear that *he himself* is the cause of the misfortune which befell the son who was expelled from his family. He comes right out and says it: "Do not think that I have come to bring peace to the earth; I have not come to bring peace, but a sword" (Matt 10:34). Swords, of course, cleave things in two, namely, they divide families. The fundamental family relationships of parents and children are destroyed:

> For I have come to set a man against his father,
> and a daughter against her mother,
> and a daughter-in-law against her mother-in-law.

All possible relationships in an extended family are cut asunder. Note the summary statement that "one's foes will be members of *one's own household.*" Jesus then speaks a frightening challenge: "Whoever loves father or mother more than me is not worthy of me; and whoever loves son or daughter more than me is not worthy of me; and whoever does not take up the cross and follow me is not worthy of me." Clearly the man expelled has proved "worthy" of Jesus, "worthy" being a clear synonym for "honor." The man expelled has chosen to look good in "God's eyes," not those of his family and village.

When we hear Luke 6:20–23 along with Luke 12:22–31, Jesus' words are pronounced with distinctive clarity and compassion. He means what he says; and he knows the consequences of his words. Jesus knows that if the expulsion has already happened, the exiled disciple needs much support, which we should hear in his voice. If the words are a caution to those risking their family's ire, then they sound differently, supportive, but cautionary. Imagining this scene will surely draw us back to 6:20–23, which is a good thing. Each one gives meaning to the other; they continue to describe the story of a disciple who has paid a great price for Jesus and his Kingdom. So in contemplating them, one should be prepared to see men and women truly shocked. The are expelled from their world of security and meaning. Is there any comfort for them? Who might approach them, offer them something, look them in the eye? How long will the crisis go on?

Contemplation 5: Watching and Hearing Jesus Teach His "Way" (Mark 8:31—10:52)

Jesus begins a journey from Caesarea Philippi to Jerusalem, which is continually narrated in Mark 8:31—10:52. We know that the word "way" can simply refer to a journey, but as well as to a pattern of behavior. Christianity was often called "the Way": Saul sought to bring any who belonged to the Way to Jerusalem (Acts 9:2); Paul confessed, "I admit to you, that according to the Way, I worship the God of our ancestors" (Acts 24:14). On the way (Mark 8:31—10:52) to Jerusalem, Jesus continuously taught the disciples his "way" of thinking and acting, a coherent series of instructions. This "Way" of Jesus is expressed in eight consecutive scenes along the way.

First Description of "the Way" (8:34–38)

Being acclaimed as God's prophet and Anointed One seems not to matter to Jesus because he immediately silences this sort of speech: "And he sternly ordered them not to tell anyone about him" (Mark 8:30). In place of this honorific speech, Jesus proclaims the opposite, namely, his coming shame at the hands of Jerusalem's leaders (and his vindication by God). Peter rebukes Jesus for this (accepting shame, in place of honor), and is in turn rebuked, i.e., shamed by Jesus: "You do not think the thoughts of God, but human thoughts." Now the teacher teaches his "way." This, once more, is a world upside down.

"All who want to be my followers, let them deny themselves, take up their cross and follow me." If anyone wants to be my follower, then they must walk in my "way." "Deny yourself" simply means to *not-strive for honor in men's eyes*, to *not-climb the ladder of public approval*, to *not-play aggressive games*. Jesus did not play them, and his disciples must forsake them also. "Take up one's cross" refers, not to pain and suffering, but to how "cross" was understood, namely, as consummate shame: "He despised the shame of the cross" (Heb 12:1–2). All honor, then, is to look good in God's eyes, as Jesus always seeks to do, "thinking the thoughts of God." This colors how we understand "Those who want to save their life will lose it, and those who lose their life for my sake, and for the sake of the gospel, will save it." Instead of "life" read "honor." If one pursues honor in the eyes of one's peers, one forfeits honor in God's eyes. Furthermore, what could be more honorable than "gaining the whole world," riches, power, grandeur, elegance, etc.—honorable in human eyes, but hardly in God's eyes. The "way" of Jesus, on the contrary, includes mockery by humans because disciples seek honor only in God's eyes, that is, they follow Jesus on "his way." As always, see the faces. How does Jesus hold his head, how do the disciples hold theirs? What is Jesus' delivery like? Can you imagine the emotions in each disciple who hears this? What do the disciples do after hearing this?

Second Description of "the Way" (9:14–27)

Juxtaposed with the wonder of the metamorphosis of Jesus is the failure of his disciples to understand anything: "They kept the matter to themselves, questioning what this rising from the dead could mean" (Mark 9:10). But they just witnessed the honor of Jesus and God's valedictory of him?! They rejoin the other disciples, who have gotten into an argument with the Scribes, who seem to have gotten the better of it. For, a father brought his son to them to cure him, but they tried and failed. Unlike their teacher, they are powerful neither in word or deed. Surely this means shame in the eyes of the crowd. The father rehearses the degree of his son's illness—this is indeed a severe illness—concluding with the complaint that the disciples were unable to heal the son. The son then demonstrates on his own the severity of his sickness, which, the father says, he has had from childhood ("from childhood" means incurable, like "blind from birth"). A hard case, indeed. "If you can do anything, pity us and help us." Jesus' response does not sound very sympathetic: "All things are possible to him who believes," to which the father responds, "I do believe, help my unbelief." Jesus now is in total control. After another demonstration of the severity of the illness, Jesus overpowers the demon responsible for it and "it came out of him." Of course, Jesus is empowered to work such healings, but the disciples are still shamed that they tried and failed. Were they presumptuous? arrogant? seeking honor in the eyes of the crowd—all likely options, given their consistent failure to learn Jesus' "way"? They would be successful, Jesus says, if they sought the power and mercy of God in prayer, rather than acting on their own. "All things are possible" applies also to them, but only in prayer to God, because all honor is owed God.

Imagine the whole string of events. Watch the disciples try to heal the boy but fail. Are they embarrassed? How many times did they try? Imagine Jesus' effect on the father and son when he appears. Imagine the convulsed boy. Read the father's face when he petitions Jesus. Finally, discern the expression of Jesus' face and the tone of his voice when he sets the disciples straight.

Third Description of "the Way" (9:32–37)

Not only did they ignore Jesus' second repetition of his "way" (Mark 9:31–32), but the disciples return to the honor battles typical of their village, jockeying for status and respect: "On the way they argued with one another who was the greatest" (Mark 9:34). Their "silence" = admission of folly. What is "the way" of Jesus here? "Whoever wants to be first must be last of all and servant of all." First, of course, but last? Never! What folly! Jesus brings into their midst a child, not because the child exemplified innocence, but because the child is the most honor-less creature imaginable.

Why "honor-less"? Children in that world tended to die young (1/3 of those born in the same year are dead by six years old). They were trained from infancy to assume chores, not preside like princes, whose every wish is honored. They are nobodies in their families. They serve elders and they obey commands (today children give adults commands); they are never spoiled. They embody the calculus of honor that forms the "way of Jesus": least is greatest; last is first. St. Paul uses the same calculus to describe the "way" of Jesus: "Christ, the power of God and the wisdom of God. For God's foolishness is wiser than human wisdom, and God's weakness is stronger than human strength" (1 Cor 1:24–25). What does honor look like in God's eyes:

> Not many of you were wise by human standards, not many were powerful, not many were of noble birth. But God chose what is foolish in the world to shame the wise; God chose what is weak in the world to shame the strong; God chose what is low and despised in the world, things that are not, to reduce to nothing things that are. (1 Cor 1:27–29).

The honor-less child is the poster figure for Jesus' "way." How shameful, then, that an honor-less child has more honor than the adult disciples. Do you still need clues on how to imagine this scene?

Fourth Description of "the Way" (9:38–41)

John the disciple reports to Jesus that "We saw someone casting out demons in your name, and we tried to stop him, because he was not following us." This sounds like the exchange between John the Baptizer and his disciples over the success of Jesus (John 3:25–30). Both sets of disciples, it seems, view the world in terms of a "zero sum game": there is only so much honor and respect in the world, so that an interloper who succeeds must be taking honor and respect from the master or teacher. Neither Jesus nor the Baptizer think this way. Since "the way" of both eschews pursuit of fame in human eyes, they do not see themselves diminished by the success of another, since these others are doing just what their masters were doing. "He must increase, I must decrease" (John 3:30). Jesus defuses the anger of his disciple with a lesser remark: "Do not stop him; for no one who does a deed of power in my name will be able soon afterward to speak evil of me" (9:38–39). We are not in competition; we are not trying to gain honor and we are not harmed by another's success.

Fifth Description of "the Way" (10:1–12)

Jesus enters Judea, presumably hostile territory, and is immediately challenged by Pharisees over the issue of divorce. We focus less on the "dogma" of divorce and view the scene as one more attempt to "test Jesus," so as to dishonor and discredit him. The weapons are contrasting pieces of the Scriptures, the Pharisees citing Moses (Deut 24:1–4) and Jesus repeating God's words to Adam (Gen 2:18, 23–25). No contest, for surely the very word of God in Genesis trumps anything said ages later by Moses. Moreover, the default for Jesus and the early church is to go to *the earliest parts of Scripture* as being more significant than later parts. Moses approved of divorce because of the hardness of human hearts. What is not discussed are the social reasons for a divorce (see *Cameo 21*, below). But winning once more is hardly the point, for Jesus wins all such challenges. He and the disciples leave the public scene and rewind the tape of the discussion. Now Jesus says something different to them in private: he puts to them a *legal case*: a man who divorces and remarries another, commits adultery. What is *not* discussed is the case of the person who is divorced by another, that is, the victim of the situation. But this begs the social issue: what does divorce mean in that culture? A man would most likely divorce so as to make a more advantageous match, i.e., gain a spouse of greater social standing and wealth. Hence, divorce is another example of seeking honor, fame and respect. Divorce for this reason contradicts "the Way" of Jesus which challenges such thinking and behavior. And so this reason for divorce contradicts Jesus' "way." This is a social reason, not a moral one. In the following cameo, note that only "wealth" (i.e., the goods of the betrothal contract) are in view.

Cameo 21: An Actual Divorce Decree (only about finances)

To: Protarchus

From: Zois, daughter of Heraclides, along with her guardian and brother, Irenaeus, son of Heraclides; and from Antipater, son of Zenon.

Zois and Antipater agree that they have separated from one another, dissolving the union that they have formed on the basis of an agreement made through the same tribunal in Hathyr of this 17th year of Caesar.

And Zois acknowledges that she has received from Antipater by hand from his house the material that he received as dowry: clothing valued at 120 drachmai and a pair of gold earrings.

The marriage agreement shall from now on be nullified; and neither Zois nor anyone acting on her behalf shall initiate proceedings against Antipater for restitution of the dowry; nor shall either person initiate proceedings against the other concerning cohabitation or any issue whatsoever up to the present. And subsequently it shall be lawful for Zois to marry another man and for Antipater to marry another woman without either of them being answerable.

In addition to this agreement being valid, whoever transgresses it shall be liable both for damages and the prescribed fine.

17th year of Caesar, Pharmouthi 2.

(see www.kchanson.com/ANCDOCS/greek/divorce.html)

Sixth Description of "the Way" (10:17–22)

A man with "many possessions" asks Jesus a question, which seems neutral and not challenging: "Good Teacher, what must I do to inherit eternal life." Like all people in that culture, Jesus deflects compliments because they put him in another's debt. Hence, he rejects the compliment, saying "No one is good but God." But he answers the question, by repeating the obvious, *The Commandments*. One keeps them not to gain respect, but to honor God. Yes, says the man, I have done such since my youth, signaling that he is a good person, to whom Jesus responds with "love." Jesus' "Way," however, is not that of wealth, respect, and honor in peoples' eyes, and so he invites the man to come and follow him in a non-honorable way by foreswearing all possessions and so foregoing the status and respect that they reflect. What shame would come upon this man! He will not be able to arrange for favorable marriages for his children—without wealth, that is; what of his house, possessions, land, etc.—all signs of his honor in the eyes of the village. To sell and *give* these away to the poor is insanity; *lend*, maybe, which loans would be repaid. But to *give* to those who will *not* repay you *nor* restore your fortune is unthinkable. Jesus is asking the man to commit social suicide.

What is wrong with this picture? Jesus' invitation is foolish in the extreme, shameless, and idiotic. The man reacted properly according to his culture: he was "shocked and went away grieving." Yes, the root of all evil is money, because it leads to pride, which inevitably leads to a passion for honor and respect. Jesus declares this as a formal part of his "Way": "How hard it will be for those who have wealth to enter the kingdom of God!" On their own, the disciples cannot reach this, but as Jesus says, "For mortals it is impossible, but not for God." Success rests only in God; and success is dependent on Jesus' "Way" of non-honor. Note that "success" in God's eyes means "ruin" in men's eyes. Imagine the wealth of this man, his clothing, his demeanor, his self-assurance. Does he think he is a "good" man? Is he prideful when he says that he has kept the Commandments from his youth? Why does Jesus "look at him and love him"? Watch both faces when Jesus invites him to sell all and give it away. How long before the shock starts? See the man walk away.

Seventh Description of "the Way" (10:28–31)

Peter challenges Jesus with his question, "What about us?"—hardly a neutral remark. Jesus just used a simile to show how difficult it is for a rich man to enter the Kingdom by comparing him to a camel loaded with merchandise trying to squeeze through a narrow passage. Now he resorts to hyperbole again to answer the "What about me?" question. *A hundred fold!* Outrageous, who needs a hundred fathers, a hundred mothers, a hundred boats, a hundred houses, and a hundred fields? This really means a hundred headaches. The very excess promised is Jesus' shaming response to the foolish question. The disciples, moreover, would resemble the rich man who just walked away, who could not give up his wealth. Moreover, an overload of possessions and kin means that all of one's time would be spent attending to them; what about the kingdom? A "return" to those who previously "left all for my sake and the sake of the gospel" would not be a reward of honor, but a burden, a stumbling block, and a failure, not in the eyes of others, but in God's and Jesus' eyes. The hyperbole confounds the calculus of the disciples. They do not win the LOTTO and return super rich to their old lives. Respect for service is the *honor* that God bestows, not the material success which impresses others on earth.

Eighth Description of "the Way" (10:35–45)

True to form, the disciples do not comprehend the third announcement of Jesus' forthcoming mockery and humiliation (Mark 10:33–34). In fact James and John challenge Jesus by requesting just the opposite and so two "Ways" are thus contrasted, his and theirs. The brothers wait until the others leave to ask of Jesus for the highest possible honor: "Grant us to sit, one at your right hand and one at your left, in your glory." So much for his teaching on "the Way." Instead of granting this, Jesus offers them a distinctive share in his Way, rejection and loss of honor: "Are you able to drink the cup that I drink, or be baptized with the baptism that I am baptized with?" His question to them is a counter challenge, which they foolishly accept! "We can!" "Drink the cup" refers to the tradition of drinking a cup of sorrow and humiliation to the dregs. And "baptism," according the original meaning of the verb, means grinding something to dust, reducing it to nothing. Thus sharing Jesus' cup and baptism means sharing in his mockery and humiliation, his nothingness. Jesus offers the brothers another crack at following his "Way." But only God bestows genuine honor. So, instead of session at Jesus' hands, James and John receive a share of his mockery, but hardly a voluntary one. The other disciples are quick to pick up on the arrogance of the two brothers, and a fight begins; "zero sum game" again—there is only so much favor and benefaction from Jesus, and the two brothers are perceived as trying to gain it all. The rest think they are losing. Jesus, however, calls off the fight by telling all the disciples that they cannot be people of status and power—on the contrary. Disciples must follow his rule: "Whoever wishes to become great among you must be your servant, and whoever wishes to be first among you must be slave of all." This, then, perfectly summarizes "the Way" of Jesus (Mark 10:43–44). Moreover, Jesus never tells others to do what he himself does not do; so he continues with reference to himself: "For the Son of Man came not to served, but to serve and give his life as ransom for many" (Mark 10:45).

The way to Jerusalem is over. The "way" of Jesus has been taught. It remains for Jesus to model this "way" by his behavior during the next week.

7

Did Jesus Laugh?
Did He Make Others Laugh?

And Now from "Comedy Central" . . .

In the last chapter we began to hear Jesus speak, which required both imaginative scenarios for the eyes and itching ears to hear all that was being said in Jesus' own culture. Because we tend to take Jesus very seriously, it is easy to imagine Jesus, the Teacher, teaching "a new teaching, with authority." We might imagine him as a serious speaker of important words, delivered in a grave manner – as a preacher or politician would. But Jesus often spoke in different keys, stuff that was at first glance not at all "serious" or "profound." Jesus was also a word-wizard: he told stories, he played with words which have double meanings, he told puns, cracked jokes, and even publicly turned the tables on those who tried to trap him in his speech. Now we want to imagine him telling stories, which are called "parables."

The default of modern hearers/readers imaging these stories is to make Jesus sound serious, grave, "religious," or "theological." If by "serious" we mean, words of great importance, we would be correct. But to imagine that he told them in a "serious" manner is quite another thing. Everything he spoke was important, but not everything was delivered with gravity. In the cultural world of Jesus, we must set our hearing free to go in different directions. Does your imagination allow Jesus to be an entertainer? Someone from "Comedy Central?" Do you imagine Jesus himself laughing and enjoying making others laugh? This is what we have to imagine here.

To "hear" Jesus himself laugh and make others laugh, we need to pause to make sure we have the right jargon for this. The Greek words for "to laugh" or "laughter" are very few, the most common one being *gelao*. While it has synonyms, this is far and away the primary Greek word/verb. Yet the Greeks laughed a lot; after all, they invented comedy. The grand-daddy of Greek lexica for the New Testament define laughter as arising from three different scenarios: 1. laughter directed against some person as a form of ridicule; 2. laughter resulting from seeing some humorous event or as the result of listening to a humorous account; and 3. laughter which reflects happiness and joy. Let's imagine what this looks like.

Cameo 22: What Did Laughter Mean in Jesus' Culture?

Meaning 1: Laughter as ridicule:
"The Lord laughs at the wicked, for he sees that their day is coming."
 (Ps 37:13)
"The unrighteous show contempt, but the Lord will laugh them to scorn."
 (Wis 4:18)
"The couriers went from city to city . . . but those to whom they were sent
 laughed them to scorn, and mocked them." (2 Chr 30:10)

Meaning 2: Laughter because of "humorous" seeing and hearing:
 Be patient, for this is the laughter of the parables, to be discussed later.

Meaning 3: Sorrow turned into Laughter
"He will fill your mouth with laughter, and your lips with shouts of joy."
 (Ps 8:21)
"Those who sow in tears reap with shouts of joy. Those who go out weeping,
 bearing the seed for sowing, shall return with shouts of joy, carrying their
 sheaves." (Ps 126:5)
"How honored are you who mourn, for you will laugh for joy." (Luke 6:21)

Even so, how do we imagine that Jesus laughed? What characterized his humorous stories? And what in the stories made others laugh? In the late nineteenth century, a picture of Jesus laughing (*Jesu qui rire*) caused a sensation, indicating that Christians never imagined him laughing. So, this might be a difficult imaginative scenario for people whose Jesus is as grave as a Roman senator. But a quick glance at the Bible and at stories about Jesus should free us to imagine "laughter" in the Scriptures.

To Laugh or not to Laugh: Who Would not Laugh at These Stories?

Could the audience *not* laugh when Ehud, a judge, gets a private audience with King Eglon, who is then sitting on his toilet. His bowels moved in several senses, one of which was because Ehud thrust a hidden sword into the king's bowels and everything flowed out (Judg 3:15–25). Are hearers meant to laugh when they recall the spat over whether Sarah "laughed"? When she heard that she would become pregnant, "She laughed." When called to account, Sarah said, "I did not laugh." Husband Abraham got the last word: "You lied." Does this at least make us a smile? Should we laugh at King Ahaz, who failed to persuade Naboth to sell him his vineyard—a king, with real power rendered powerless, who turns his face to the wall and mopes. But Ahaz's queen, Jezebel, laughs at this weak king and takes matters into her own hands, a supposedly weak gender, doing a man's job! How should we react to Ahaz?

Jesus himself was a superb word-smith, whose facility needs to be recognized to hear in full what he wanted to say. Imagine a scene where a Pharisee, a "teacher of Israel," sneaks out at night to talk to Jesus and begins by insulting him with the luke-warm remark: "We know that you are a teacher sent from God," an insult because it admits so very little. Jesus hears the insult and responds by playing a word game with Nicodemus, using double-meaning words to stump him. Just as Nicodemus insulted Jesus as "teacher of Israel," Jesus now returned the compliment: "Are you a teacher of Israel, and yet you do not understand these things?" (John 3:10). When the Pharisee hears "You must be born anothen," which could mean either "again" or "from above," he opts for the literal meaning, mocking Jesus as demanding that he squeeze back into his mother's womb. We laugh at how silly Nicodemus' remark was and how Jesus then hoisted him on his own petard. Is it funny when John and James furtively ask Jesus for a special favor, which everyone knows is the poison gas of envy. How much more laughable is the version of this same story when their mother replaces them and she herself pleads their cause (Matt 20:20–23)? Of course it is laughable to hear the man-born-blind reduce to babble the powerful and wise Pharisees in John 9. Finally, consider the puzzle Jesus puts before his hostile audience in Mark 12: 35–37. Jesus asked, "How can the scribes say that the Messiah is the son of David? David himself, by the Holy Spirit, declared, 'The Lord said to my Lord, 'Sit at my right hand, until I put your enemies under your feet.' David himself calls him Lord; so how can he be his son?'" If Jesus's opponents were put on the spot, remember that "a large crowd was listening to him with delight." Jesus laughed and made his audience laugh. We cannot hear Jesus and not listen to the humor in the narrative.

I imagine, moreover, Jesus also on occasion "played" with his disciples. Peter asked what reward he and the Eleven would get for "leaving everything" to follow Jesus—a laughable question, which Jesus mocks with great hyperbole: "Everyone who has left houses or brothers or sisters or father or mother or children or fields, for my name's sake, will receive a hundredfold" (Matt 19:29). A ridiculous answer to an impertinent question! Think about it. Who needs the burden of 100 of everything, including mothers-in-law. Imagine two disciples on their way to Emmaus, heavy with grief and frustration, who do not recognize Jesus as he draws near. We, however, see what they do not see, namely, Jesus in a very playful mood, searching for his lost sheep, playing an unfamiliar role, a guy who does not know what is going on. We hear the respectful, but teasing way Jesus asks them what they are talking about. Cleopas totally misreads the scene and reproaches the traveler: "Are you the only person in Jerusalem who does not know the things that just happened there?" The audience hearing this story surely laughs at the irony of the situation, not at the disciples, but at the clever and humorous way Jesus turns sorrow into joy and tears into smiles. Other examples? Remember how Simon Peter, set free from prison by an angel, went to a safe house, knocked for entry, only to find that the gate of this house is locked to him because all inside knew that the real Simon Peter was in jail (Acts 12:12-17). Call it sarcasm, but isn't it funny when Paul tells some Galatians, who are enamored of circumcision ("cutting around"), to "cut it off" entirely (Gal 5). People in the Bible laugh all the time. It is eminently imaginable. They played with words and made each other laugh. God help the boring hearers/readers who don't get it!

Jesus Told Parables . . . and Made People Laugh

What's a "parable"? How does it work? What is supposed to happen? These were not matters of importance to Jesus' audience, who were raised on humorous stories. They knew what was funny; they knew when to laugh. But now we seem to need scholars to tell us what Jesus' audience automatically understood. It gets worse: there is an ancient saying: "two rabbis, three opinions," that is, "two scholars talking about parables, three opinions." Our scholars battle to establish a definitive way of hearing parables, which Jesus did not have to do with his audience. So, when we want to make an imaginative scenario of Jesus telling "parables," we want to hear them as did the first audiences. Because they heard parables so often, they developed a mental image of what typically goes on in a parable.

Cameo 23: How to Hear a Parable

1. Jesus was an *Entertainer*, who made people laugh; he teased them with puzzles and riddles (see Mark 12:42–47). Verbal games were the primary entertainment of the ancients (ever hear of Samson's riddle or the riddle of the Sphinx?). 2. A *parable* makes *one and only one point*; which 99% of the time is about a person, the rest are stage props. 3. Always ask *"What's wrong with this picture?"* If you are not shocked, you do not understand this "high context culture." 4. With a peasant audience, *agriculture* is a most appropriate backdrop for Jesus's parables: sowing, harvesting, separating wheat from chaff, vineyards, orchards and day laborers. 5. True parables *turn the world upside down*: foolishness is wisdom in a topsy-turvy world (see 1 Cor 1:25). 6. Most parables focus on a *central figure*, who according to the story is the most dishonorable, the most foolish, the weakest person imaginable. 7. Jesus eventually *shuts up*, which means that his audience must now wrestle with what he said. Funny stories becomes *riddles to be solved*.

Maybe we need a *Parables for Dummies* to make the obvious obvious. It would contain the following info: a parable is a *narrative* told about *someone*, whose *behavior is so bizarre* and so far from the common sense of the audience, that the hearers *react* to the story with laughter at the contrast of the story with their experience. The audience, moreover, knew to focus on the *central figure*, the protagonist, not the rest of the cast. They expected Jesus to tell stories about things familiar to their world. They presumed—rightly—that Jesus would *know his audience*. For example, since they were all village peasants, and "peasant farmers," it is hardly surprising that Jesus talked the language of "agriculture," that is, about farmers and fields, sowing, harvesting gathering into barns, kinds of seed, day laborers on someone's fields.

Living in a *"high context"* world, Jesus' peasant audience knew the relative size of typical plots, the devastation wrought by drought, how many oxen were needed to plow a field, how many sheep and goats a household would likely have, etc. They did not need to imagine all this, because it was part of their experience. They all had intimate knowledge of one another's *taxes, debts, and land foreclosure*. They knew that occasionally the whole family of a debtor was sold into slavery to pay the un-payable debt. This was public business known by all, with accompanying shame, because it effected the value of dowries, bride-prices, wedding feasts, etc. The audience already knew how the stories worked and what to laugh at, as well as the universal conclusion that for the audience the protagonist was: "What a crazy farmer!" "What a stupid shepherd!" "What a cowardly landowner!" They knew this because they compared what Jesus was saying with what they knew about how a peasant's world actually worked. They instinctively knew that Jesus was telling stories that were simply crazy, zany, "over the top," and exaggerated. They could not define "hyperbole," but they knew it when they heard it.

They *laughed, howled, and hooted*, because Jesus set out to make them laugh, which was not difficult to do. Therefore, they did not need *Parables for Dummies* because they simply knew all of this first hand. Moreover, the audience did not need footnotes, because everything narrated had an immediate connection with what they already knew. For example, they knew the value of a flock of 100 sheep (Luke 15:2-4).

They had, moreover, *imaginations to phastasize the life of the rich and powerful*, such as the "a rich man dressed in purple and fine linen who feasted sumptuously every day" (Luke 16:19); or the king's wedding banquet for his son: "I have prepared my dinner, my oxen and my fat calves have been slaughtered, and everything is ready" (Matt 22:4). They could imagine huge sums of money, such as five, two (Luke 19) and 500 talents (Matt 18:24). They could imagine the good life of the absentee landlord living in the city off the produce of his country estates. Even peasants in the Land of Little could image life in the elite Kingdom of Plenty and Power. Jesus did not have to teach an audience how to listen to a "parable."

So, it is both important to appreciate that Jesus was a born natural entertainer. He did not study "comedy" in college or go to the Yale Drama School. But he surely learned what a clever speaker said and did. He learned to "deliver." We would rightly compare him with a person who had formal speech training. Imagine a Roman senator standing before his peers, whose "delivery" had to be grave, formal, careful and calculating. Voice: he was taught how to use his voice: when to be loud or soft, rapid or slow, when to pause. For him, everything was highly calculated. While gestures were officially rare, facial expressions were encouraged, such as raising eyebrows, frowning, sneering, and the like. We imagine this noble Roman as a person who takes himself seriously. He speaks to persuade, not to entertain. He wants respect, not laughter.

Jesus did not know any such theory. But we imagine that he learned dramatic delivery both from observing other speakers and from his own development as a public speaker, i.e., what worked. Given the humorous nature of Jesus's preferred speech act, the parable, we expect that he developed *delivery* appropriate to his topic: 1. He would *play the character* of the person being described or speaking; 2. he would surely *accompany* the story with *body language*; 3. since he was not a formal person, but an entertainer, we imagine he assumed varied *postures* (standing, leaning, bending), modulated the *tone and speed* of his speech; 4. he constantly changed *facial expressions*, and "talked with his hands." We imagine his *delivery* as the medium which fits the message: "When you're smiling, the whole world smiles with you; when you're crying . . ." If we imagine that Jesus laughed when he told his laughable stories, then he himself laughed so as to make his audience laugh.

The Kingdom Is Heaven Is Like . . .

Let's start easy. Let's imagine "parables," that is, funny stories, with few complications. But "imagining" will mean that we have to do two things at the same time. First, like the audience, we need to imagine how agriculture actually worked, the kind of scenarios we imagined in the first part of this book. Then we have to imagine how wacky is the story that Jesus actually tells, what is crazy about it? foolish? "over the top," or "hyperbolic." This will be hard for us because our default is to take everything Jesus says literally and as factually truthful. We honestly do not realize that he is "pulling our leg." If we can imagine the typical world of Jesus and his audience, as well as the whacky distortion of this in Jesus' story, we will begin to hear what Jesus wanted to say.

The Foolish Farmer (Mark 4:1–9)

The first parable narrated in the collections of parables assembled by Mark, Matthew and Luke is the story of a genuinely foolish farmer. Mark says to imagine Jesus in a boat just off the beach (sound travels excellently over water); with so much sand around, we might also imagine Jesus picks up a handful of sand. The audience is mostly farmers, with some fishermen (i.e., the boat); and Jesus plays to this audience. He talks agriculture, but not the kind they know. A Sower went out to sow. OK We get the scenario. But he immediately acts like an amateur or a foolish farmer. Jesus, always good with gestures and body language, acts out the role of "foolish farmer";

when he tosses some sand over there, gulls and crows swoop down to see if it is edible. Natural, but what is not natural is a farmer intentionally throwing a fourth of his seed on paths packed down by many feet, where only scavenger birds will benefit from it. Second, Jesus throws more sand onto the stones on the shore; but there is little or no soil there, so the seed is fated to die of thirst. The audience is really into it now, for they guffaw and howl with laughter at the foolishness of this hapless farmer. This man is an idiot! Still, Jesus tosses more sand into some brambles, which all know will smother a good part of the crop. Can it get much zanier? Jesus' gesture of tossing sand and predicting its fate are immediately appreciated by his peasant audience, who double over with uncontrollable laughter. But, Jesus tosses the last of the sand on ground ready for a new crop. When Jesus says that this quarter of the seed will "grow up and increase and yield thirty and sixty and a hundredfold" (Mark 4:8), they keep laughing because the result in pure fantasy. And besides, it is funny to see this farmer succeed through no fault of his own. Once the audience measures the parable beside what it knows of agriculture, the fun begins and Jesus makes them laugh with gusto. They know something we do not know. Maybe we need a cameo on basic agriculture in Jesus' time?

Cameo 24: A Peasant's View of Agriculture

1. *Land*: family owned, primary source of "wealth," 2. *Size*: very small plots, 5 hectares will feed one family; half of field lies fallow annually 3. *Quality of soil*: inferior because good land expropriated by rich and powerful. 4. *Method*: sow, then plough with oxen (with-iron tipped plow, shallow plowing); constant weeding needed. 5. *Obstacles*: scant rain at best (Tiberias had 11" of rain annually), but rains do not always come, then drought and famine follow; possible storms and accidental trampling of the crop. Yield: 1.5 hectares could feel one adult; the yield of 5 hectares needed for family of 2 adults and 3 children. 6. *Subsistence*: just enough for the next year, little to eat. 7. *Size of harvest*: maximum return = 5 fold, from which next-year's seed must be taken, animals fed, today's taxes paid (in kind), and barter for what farmer cannot produce, not in the farmer's interest. 8. *Crops*: mostly grain, but pressure to grow commercial crops (grapes, olives). 9. *Paid labor*: after inadequate harvest, farmer would take work on larger farms as tenant or day-laborer. 10. *Taxes*: variable, but punishing (1/3 and even 1/2); taxes cause peasant farmers to go into debt to pay. 11. *Debt*: generally unpayable, so farm might be confiscated or peasant pays off debt with work in another man's fields. See also: Cameo 6: "What's for Lunch?"; Cameo 25: Jesus' Intimate Acquaintance with and Concern for Debt; Cameo 26: Taxcollectors, Taxes, and Debt.

Let's reconsider the story from what we know about how peasants understand agriculture and how Jesus' parables generally work. To be sure, Jesus *knows his audience*: he talks agriculture, He tells them about a farmer, whose sowing is immediately recognized by all as zany. He and his audience know the uneven *quality of the land* in Galilee: some good, other dry, and much unfriendly to crops. They can imagine what a *super harvest* would look like ("the land of a rich man produced abundantly," Luke 12:16). We recognize that the story typically *progresses* from one stage of foolishness to another and still another. This is *calculated* to make the *audience smile, laugh, howl and guffaw*, the appropriate reaction. The laughter erupts because the description of the farmer is *"over-the-top," ridiculous and hyperbolic*. Even the eventual success of the farmer is laughable because it is so improbable. And so, the world of these peasants is *turned upside down*. Everything seems reversed: fools succeed where true farmers don't. Peasant farmers, who would be delighted with 5% increase in a harvest, simply cannot fathom how this consummate fool gets an outrageously large harvest: "thirty, sixty and a hundredfold." Finally, *Jesus shuts up*. No more words. He has apparently finished "teaching." them. But the *audience has to react* somehow. How long does it take them to realize that story-time and laughter are over? But what does this mean? Some get the point that this story has morphed into a riddle to unravel or a puzzle to solve. They are the ones to whom Jesus said: "Let those who have ears, let them hear."

When we grant that the world described by Jesus has been turned upside down, maybe the folly of the sower suggests the folly of another figure? The first public words Jesus, the "teacher," spoke were: "The kingdom of God has come near; repent, and believe in the good news" (Mark 1:15). Although this parable is not prefaced with "The Kingdom of Heaven is like . . ." as are many others (Mark 4:26, 30; Matt 13:24, 31, 33, 44–47), should we imagine that this "teaching" is about anything or anybody else? Just what is this teacher teaching? So, those who have ears to hear have some clues to solve the riddle. Who or what is important in Jesus' life? One person only, but could Jesus liken a "foolish father" to his Father? What would it mean to suppose that the "foolish farmer" represents God? Well, let's try out this idea.

What sort of foolish thing might this God be doing? Forget agriculture, think "people." God is so interested in the welfare of the house of Israel that he sends a teacher who requires that they "repent," which literally means "change your mind." But about what? How God really acts? What God is laboring to do? What does success mean for this God? Remember that the world in Jesus' story is intentionally made topsy-turvy and upside down. What does it mean if this God never quits, despite dreadful outcomes? What kind of God thinks that "foolishness" is wisdom and "weakness" is strength" (hint: 1 Cor 1:24–25)?

What's Wrong with This Picture? (Matt 13:31–33)

A quick imagining of the scenario suggests that everything is normal. A farmer put seed into his field, which is what farmers do, and a housewife seeds her flour with leaven, as do all women making bread. But this is precisely why we need some help imagining these parables as Jesus' audience would have. Much more is happening than our modern imaginations perceive. We expect real parables to be zany, over the top; we are supposed to laugh at what is happening. What's zany here? Laughable here? Second, the behaviors described don't seem to be "over-the-top." Aren't parables suppose to make their hearers laugh? Aren't they supposed to turn the world upside down? Then to make an appropriate imaginative scenario we need more information, to try to feel about the characters and their actions, as a native would. We need help in imagining these two stories.

Here two parables are stitched together. They have to do with a gender-divided world: a male in male space, with a man doing male tasks vs. a female doing female tasks in a female space. Thus, when we then imagine these stories, noticing how they reflect a gender-divided worlds, we have our first important element in our new scenario. The "social geography" is accurate.

But something is not said in the first story about the farmer putting a mustard seed into his field. Most people imagine that it is planting time, so the farmer's field is already sown (with grain, wheat, etc.), which is already growing. Again, everything seems. But this farmer then intentionally puts a different kind of seed into the field already sown with grain. Now, bells go off! Something both wrong and foolish has happened, which the audience recognizes but we don't. First, a "mustard seed" is a noxious weed, which ought to be pulled up, not planted. And the fact that it grows so large as to house birds is even worse. This weed is competing with the crop for sunlight, moisture, etc. If it has grown so big that birds can rest in it, it now houses the enemy of the crop, for birds live by raiding the crop. So it grows abundantly, but this is a greater threat to the crop. "It grows entirely wild and when it is sown it is scarcely possible to get place free of it" (Pliny, *Natural History* 18.170). Does this farmer want a giant weed in his field? Yet he intentionally put one into his field.

Second, in the "high context" world of farmers, they know the prohibition of mixing seeds in the same field: "You shall not sow your vineyard with two kinds of seed, lest the whole yield be forfeited to the sanctuary, the crop which you have sown and the yield of the vineyard" (Deut 22:9). This same prohibition extends to the yoking of a ox with an ass (Deut 22:10), the planting of grain in a vineyard (Lev 19:19), as well as weaving the stuff of which clothing is made must be all wool or all flax (Deut 22:11). This prohibition of mixing kinds was universally recognized by all Israelites, both peasants and elites. So, what this farmer is doing appears to be both evil and foolish: evil, because it flagrantly violates the law of separation, and foolish, because the original crop "will be forfeited to the sanctuary."

Because the farmer intentionally puts the seed in his field, he appears to know what he is doing; but he just does not care or calculate. How foolish is this? What reaction would Jesus' audience likely express? This subsistence farmer has forfeited his year's entire crop; what is he and his family going to eat? And for what, so that a silly mustard seed—a noxious weed— might grow into a bush? His actions, then, are foolish beyond measure; he has ruined himself and his family; and for what? Peasants in the audience would roar with laughter at the farmer's folly. When we make an imaginative scenario of this story, we cannot do it justice without knowing what the audience knew about putting two kinds of seed in the same field and how to think about "a mustard seed."

The second story sounds OK, but again, something important is presumed and not said. In modern times we buy bread from bakeries, so we do not know what goes into making dough. Moreover, both men and women often make their own bread at home, and so have a favorable opinion of "leaven." What we are missing is the native understanding of "leaven." Everyone in the audience knew that the start of Passover began with the removal from a house of all things leavened, which are thrown out and burned ("It was two days before the Passover and the Festival of Unleavened Bread," Mark 14:1). Why cast out and burn all leavened things? The only conclusion is that they "thought" about leaven as a pollutant, something unclean which must be kept away for every other foods (if only for that festival). St. Paul, moreover, knows the same thing, for he exhorts the Corinthians to be as separate from evil as bread is from leaven:

A little yeast leavens the whole batch of dough. Clean out the old yeast so that you may be a new batch, as you really are unleavened . . . Therefore, let us celebrate the festival, not with the old yeast, the yeast of malice and evil, but with the unleavened bread of sincerity and truth (1 Cor 5:6–8; see also "the leaven" of the Pharisees, Mark 8:15).

Furthermore, this is not just an Israelite thing, because classical authors like Plutarch says that the Greeks and Romans thought the same thing about leaven. For example, "For the leaven itself is generated out of corruption and when mixed (with flour) corrupts the mass, for it (the mass) becomes slack and powerless and in general the leavened thing appears to be putrid; then, increasing, it becomes sour and corrupts the flour" (*Quaestiones romanae et graeca* 289F). They all consider "leaven" as a corrupting pollutant, an item which we have to integrate into our new imaginary scenario.

So the housewife leavens flour. Would anyone laugh? Would anyone consider this behavior over the top? But both the mustard seed story and this one about leaven are both prefaced by "The Kingdom of Heaven is like . . ." And if the previous parable depended upon the audience knowing the "high context" law of separation, why must that sort of thinking stop when the woman puts leaven into flour? These side-by-side parables are supposed to be heard as male and female versions of the same thing. And this understanding would be a significant part of the imaginative scenario of the original audience. We cannot leave this out.

When we know the Israelite law and lore about two kinds of seeds and leaven, we can see that something is wrong with this picture. To us the male and female actions seem innocent, but not to the audience of Jesus. The shock comes when the hearers re-hear that each one says something about "the Kingdom of God." Now the world is turned upside down. These two things do NOT mix: holiness (as "separation") and pollution (as "mixing the unclean with the clean). It doesn't bother us, but it did Jesus' audience. Something is definitely wrong.

While we imagine Jesus talking, we must also imagine what effect he wanted these stories to have. How did the audience react? Laughter, of course, because the actor is doing something very foolish, to which the appropriate reaction is laughter. But Jesus becomes silent and lets the audience slip into a puzzle-solving mode. Those who have ears to hear will remember how the telling of all the parables was prefaced by "The kingdom of heaven is like . . ." What does "Kingdom of heaven" have to do with putting two kinds of seed in one field, or putting leaven into flour? Are we to suppose that the "holy"God is himself inserting the hateful seed into a field? Knowing what they knew about "leaven," how is inserting it into pure flour "like the Kingdom of Heaven"? But we have several ways to consider this: first, compare what the protagonists are doing here with what they do in the other parables in Matthew 13. Second, is this mixing of saint and sinner reflected anywhere in Jesus' own praxis? Does he eat with tax-collectors and sinners? With Romans and Gentiles?

Thus, if we want to imagine scenarios like a native, we need to come up to speed with the things they knew, but which nobody thought essential to write down. This is what all of them knew, so they did not need footnotes. If the stories do not turn your world topsy-turvy, go back and read them again.

Everything Is Wrong Here (Luke 15:1–32)

Luke tells three parables in a row, which taken as a whole provide a commentary for each other. If you get one, you get the others. Moreover, Luke himself provides a theme for these three parables, which functions like a topic sentence: "Now all the tax collectors and sinners were coming to listen to him. And the Pharisees and the scribes were grumbling and saying, 'This fellow welcomes sinners and eats with them.'" So, we have a good idea of the dramatic scenario for all three parables. This challenge to Jesus must be answered, which it is three times. But it is doubtful that Jesus spoke all three parables at one time and in one particular context. Each story should be listened to on its own terms. Evangelists, however, love to put like stuff together.

The Dumb Shepherd! We are not pastoral people; we do not tend sheep, nor have we a peasant's calculus. Modern readers, moreover, automatically tend to applaud the exceptional concern and tenderness of the shepherd searching for the lost sheep. But in the "high context" world of Jesus's peasant audience, this shepherd sounds like a first- class idiot. Let's re-hear the parable, noting "what's wrong" here, the stuff his audience would catch. 1. Leave 99 perfectly good sheep untended? 2. Search for a single lost one until it is found? This might take days, and what of the well being of the 99 in the meantime? 3. Putting it on his shoulders? Foolishness, because their shepherds would most likely break one of its legs so it cannot wander again! Their shepherds would just kick it until it rejoined the flock. 4. Furthermore, this shepherd goes home, not back to the abandoned flock; 5. he celebrates when he should be working. 6. Who's protecting the 99 sheep back on the hillside from predators and thieves? This shepherd does everything wrong! Not even close! What crazy person is Jesus speaking about?

So the audience begins to laugh and then to howl at the absurd behavior of this "shepherd," who does everything wrong. The audience knows what true shepherds do, but the one Jesus describes is beyond foolish; he is simply zany. Imagine Jesus acting out the part of this shepherd; he is having fun and they are laughing. Give this man an Emmy! But he suddenly stops speaking. He stands up straight, closes his lips and looks at his audience. What's happening now? His "silence" is also speech. And his "silence" should have an effect on the audience. All of a sudden, his "parable" has become a "riddle" or "puzzle." He has done his job, now they should do theirs. But what are they supposed to do? First, Jesus made them laugh at a parable which was hyperbolic, the proper response to which is laughter. But the world of Jesus' "silence" does not warrant laughter. What are they think? Are there some clues handy?

Disciples were once accused of "turning the world upside down" (Acts 17:6). According to the normal world, they think and act abnormally. And for Jesus' disciples this is good. After all, Jesus told people to "change your minds" (Mark 1:15); and we know that the word simply means "think differently." So, the ordinary is replaced by the out-of-the-ordinary. What was foolish might be wise; what was weak might be strong. So, let's imagine something topsy-turvy. Skip the idea that Jesus is teaching a new, better way for tending a flock of sheep. What if everything we used to think was wrong with this picture is actually right? What if "shepherd" is code for Chief Shepherd (David was a Shepherd; God in heaven is Israel's Shepherd). Skip David! If Jesus is this Shepherd, it is only because Jesus, the local shepherd, acts as the delegate of the Shepherd-of-Shepherds. "Shepherd" = God?! Now what's wrong with this parable? After the surprise, we have a riddle or puzzle which will explain the shepherd's strange behavior. Is it possible that in the new world proclaimed by Jesus, the person in charge of the flock is really doing all the right things, although totally at odds with what his audience knows? So, those who wrestled with the riddle might conclude that Jesus is describing someone who legitimates this topsy-turvy world.

Luke provides another clue to this reading in the way he presented the story: "Now all the tax-collectors and sinners came near to listen to him.

The Pharisees and the scribes grumbled and said: 'This fellow welcomes sinners and eats with them'" (Luke 15:1–2). So, the story is supposed to reply to this criticism. Not with a logical argument, but with a foolish story. Jesus (and maybe someone else) is as foolish as the zany shepherd in the story!" The alchemy here is to turn "foolishness" into "wisdom" and turn the world on its head. Jesus = foolish shepherd, because his God is such; what is good enough for God is fine by us. So, Jesus should be praised, not blamed for "eating with tax-collectors and sinners."

The Dumb Housewife. The "shepherd" parable has a gender complement; for if males = shepherds, who are out of doors and in the open, females = wives or mothers, whose indoor domain pertains to the household. In the "high context" world everyone already knows the specific gender expectations of both males and females. Moreover, since all know that the males work in the fields in the cool of the morning and return home for the main meal at midday, everyone is wondering why this woman isn't preparing that meal, the main meal of the day? Why is she spending all morning sweeping her very small house, and for a lost piece of her dowry? The hungry men will not be amused; they will scorn her, while the audience laughs. Like the story of Peter's mother-in-law getting up to serve her son-in-law and the other males (Mark 1:31) and Martha's perfectly reasonable complaint that Mary's place is in the kitchen helping her prepare food for the male guests (Luke 10: 40), Jesus' audiences know the standard household duties of females. Therefore, they laugh at the foolishness of this woman. They know the way the world should be, not the upside-down world described by Jesus.

But if the solution to the riddle of the foolish shepherd has to do with Jesus' new upside down world, especially where it is "wisdom" to search for what is lost, then probably the answer to the riddle just posed about the shepherd is the same for this woman. After all, Luke stitched them together so that they could both serve as the response to the criticism that Jesus is having commerce with what is lost.

The Prodigal Father. There is a third parable, which many call "the Prodigal Son," but really is about "the Prodigal Father." In the course of the narrative we are invited to make three different imaginative scenarios. But we must distrust our inclinations to sanitize the story and make all the characters heroes. What does the audience know that we don't? Everyone there starts with the same common knowledge about how an honorable fathers should raise honorable sons. If one needs written proof, Sirach 30 instructs fathers to "whip their sons into shape" so that they do not embarrass the father when he takes them out in public, especially to the synagogue. All fathers know that if they spare the rod, they spoil the child, who will surely embarrass the father himself by the his unrestrained behavior. Well, it appears that this father did not raise his younger son well at all. Shame on the father. What's wrong with this picture? Jesus' audience knows what should be and so they can compare it with the story Jesus tells. Never forget that all of this is taking place in public; everybody sees and hears everything. 1. The son insults his father, who is still much alive, by asking in public for his inheritance (= "drop dead, dad"). 2. Any self-respecting father would chastize his son for such a public insult. 3. But, this father swallows the insult and actually gives the son his inheritance. This is zany, shameful, but very funny. 4. Since all family wealth was in land, when the father scrapes together the portion of his estate to give the son, he is making bad transactions which will only diminish the family's wealth and standing. One suspects that all of these transactions are made in haste with little concern for their effects. 5. Everyone on the scene and in the neighborhood knows what he is doing; and in their eyes he is a consummate fool and a shameless father. 6. Nobody thinks that this father is acting honorably. Thus all judge that he is weak and foolish, because he does not know how to act like a genuine father. We need to be told this explicitly, but folk in a "high context" culture world would see it immediately. 7. Foolish, but not dumb. We presume that he knows perfectly well how the son will squander his portion. Yet he gives him the goods. 8. The farewell scene is cold and empty: no "good-byes" and "good luck" and "keep in touch." No hug, no kiss. This is not how honorable fathers and sons separate. Looks very much like a funeral. By the way, we learn later that there are other children and wonder if they were present for this? Does he indulge them as well? Therefore, all know that the father has lost all respect in the eyes of his own family and his neighbors, because he does not know how to raise a son. This kind of news travels quickly and is eagerly consumed. We, of course, know the rest of the story.

So the audience laughs at the foolish father, but do any of the characters in the story concur and justify this laughter? What about the "silent majority," the servants of the household? How do they think about the younger son's return? Nothing is said in the text, but in a "high context" world, it would be safe to say that they are upset and mortified at the father's continued folly. They were present when the son embarrassed the entire household with his shameless treatment of his father. They surely felt the pinch when so much of the estate's worth was given that son. So, it is a valid part of our imaginary scenario to ask whether they were happy that the son returned? What makes us think that they are forgiving of son for the shame he brought upon the father and the estate? They obey the fathers' commands, but we should not imagine that they are happy. Moreover, they are not stupid; they know that the son was trouble then and they see no reason to think that he will not be more trouble tomorrow. Like a Greek chorus, they speak for the audience: how foolish of the father to offer blanket forgiveness to the returning son; this is consummate foolishness; it turns the world upside down. When we imagine them laughing, we are urged to laugh as well.

In a new scene to be imagined, we learn that the son begins to show some sense. He knows that his father's servants are better off than he; they eat and he starves. What he says is true, but does it justify his resolve to return home? We saw him earlier disdaining his father, but now that he is hungry he wants to act honorably toward his father: "I will get up and go to my father, and I will say to him, 'Father, I have sinned against heaven and before you; I am no longer worthy to be called your son; treat me like one of your hired hands' " (Luke 15:18–19). Jesus' audience would probably laugh at this convenient confession by a son who has all along dishonored his father. They might well ask if he is truly showing respect for his father, or is he just hungry? He might fool his foolish father, but the critical audience? Would they laugh at this convenient show of filial piety? After all, coming from him, it is over the top and worthy of ridicule.

The audience, moreover, knows how daffy the father is. They might well imagine him daily sitting outside, scanning the horizon. Does he think that his son will come back, humble himself and seek rapprochement? Does the audience think that the father has learned anything? His foolishness abides, as well as his ineptitude to deal with this son. The speck he sees on the path gets closer and materializes into his son.

The scene quickly becomes a madhouse with members of the household and neighbors running right and left. But, they are not happy to see the son; he is nothing but shame to his father and trouble for the household; he has diminished the status of his family by his greed and foolishness. Nobody, but nobody wants him back, except his foolish father. We are not explicitly told this, but in their "high context" world, this would be the proper reaction. So the father runs (patriarchs never run, for it declares that they cannot control the situation); he throws his arms around the neck of the son. Affection? Maybe. But imagine the angry servants and neighbors picking up rocks to stone the son and chase him away, which might explain why the father embraces the son to keep him from being pelted with rocks. In their eyes the son is utterly shameful and they show it by throwing rocks. Thus, in an honor-shame context, they have by no means forgiven him. Only the father is glad to see the son, no one else. What is clear is that onlookers are astounded: this should not be. How foolish can this father be? This completely upsets their world.

But what is the audience hearing and imagining? How would they react to such a scene? Do they share the reading just outlined above? In short, do they break out laughing at so foolish an interaction? In their culture this would be heard as one of the funniest, most ridiculous stories that they have ever heard. Both father and son are objects of ridicule: the father is totally incompetent, foolish beyond measure, a complete fool; and the son is the worst behaved son on record. He was ill raised and has learned no respect for his father. He proves the saying "spare the rod and spoil the child." Therefore, increasing laughter is the proper response. But the story is not over, although everything turns out as the audience predicted.

Yet the father acts still more foolishly, for he immediately reintegrates the son into the family as though nothing has happened: "Get the best robe, find the right ring, put sandals for his feet." If the father foolishly let the son go off in the first place, that is surpassed by the consummate folly of taking him back into the family without a penalty or discipline. On the contrary, the father throws a feast to honor the son. Shame is rewarded! Listeners might well say, "What, more money wasted on this miserable son?"

The party starts but an important person is not present, the other son. And nobody has come from the house to tell him about his brother's return and the imminent feast, much less invite him, which is a very shameful way to treat the only loyal son the father has. Now we have to imagine another scenario, this time out in the estate's fields. Eventually, the foolish father himself goes out to this other son working in the fields: "And pleads with him to come in and celebrate" (15:28). Don't patriarchs have servants to send? Do patriarchs "plead" and not command? But the reaction of the laboring son is important for Jesus' disciples to evaluate the story. The commandment, "Honor your father!" does not apply here, because the father is unworthy of respect; he is very wrong and foolish in every way. When this son speaks, he speaks for the audience: "For all these years I have been working like a slave for you, and I have never disobeyed your command; yet you have never given me even a young goat so that I might celebrate with my friends. But when this son of yours came back, who has devoured your property with prostitutes, you killed the fatted calf for him!" (15:29–30). Ideally a son should never sass his father, but this father is impossible. The honorable son has always acted honorably: he worked like a slave for his father, and never disobeyed his commands. But there is NO reward for this virtuous behavior. All he seems to get from the father is neglect. We imagine that the audience would approve of this son finally standing up to defend his own honor before a dishonorable parent. They would laugh to see the foolish father finally exposed as incompetent and shameless.

The father, however, has the last word: " But we had to celebrate and rejoice, because this brother of yours was dead and has come to life; he was lost and has been found." More folly, more ineptitude, more craziness? These last words of the father cancel out the other son's evaluation on the basis of justice. The father reinstates the topic of unqualified reception of evil people back into the household. This would surely provoke the audience to shouts of "Foolish!" "Unfair!" "Ridiculous!" This continues to turn the world upside down; this reverses the rule that good is rewarded and evil punished. Except not here. The father's actions continue to turn the world topsy turvy. Yet Jesus himself has a reaction, too. He becomes silent and speaks no more. If the audience can solve the riddle Jesus just presented, they can discover his reaction and evaluation. When he shuts up, the audience must examine the story, not on the basis of their natural judgment, but on that of the foolish, prodigal father may in fact have a point. It matters who has ears to hear and not just listen.

Have You No Shame? (Matt 22:1–24)

Everyone knows what is expected of honorable shepherds, housewives and fathers. But Jesus also tells stories about the elites of his world, about kings. But the drift of the story is the same: how foolish can a person be—even a king?

The people in this parable would never be seen by peasants; but they could imagine them; and so they would make their own imaginative scenario of a "fantasy world" of society's top stratum. Imagine this: a king invited his elite peers to celebrate at the wedding banquet of his, which would honor the son as well as confirm loyalty of the nobles to the king. Honor, of course, demands a wedding banquet of sumptuous plenitude.

While peasants indeed go to wedding banquets (John 2:1–10, where, not surprisingly, the wine quickly runs out), this banquet would be over the top, for it has to reflect the wealth and status of the king. Everything must be of the best quality and lots of it, for the king's honor is symbolized in the lavishness of the feast. What a surprise, then, that the king's nobles one by one turn down the invitation, and for the silliest of reasons, such as attending to business in place of showing respect for the king, tending to a farm in preference to the palace of the king. These are serious snubs, compounded when some invitees further dishonor the king by manhandling his servants and thus show contempt for the king. This gossip will spread all over the kingdom. The king's honor rating is crashing. But, how will peasants in Jesus' audience react to this scenario? With laughter, because they know that their taxes support a king who uses the same taxes to woo his nobles. They would enjoy hearing how the king's peers snub him and show him their contempt and laugh heartily the king's embarrassment. This never happens to kings! What a foolish king, who misreads the loyalty of his nobles and does not get his way. How foolish he looks. And little people love to laugh at big folk who fall down.

Who, however, will eat the banquet? Will anyone honor the king and his son? To whom can the king turn? Now calculate the folly of his next moves. First, the king sends his servants into the city, its alleys and byways, to brings peasant artisans into his palace and to seat them where the nobles would have sat. Hardly nobles, they are mere peasants. Second, Luke's account adds that these servants also went outside the city where prostitutes, thieves, unsavory people and others declared "expendable" resided; they were not even allowed in the city. They, too, are brought into the palace, seated, and fed a feast set for a king. Third, from what we know of peasants' diets, they generally ate grains and legumes, but very rarely meat; and their "bread" would be made with non-choice grains (see Cameo 6). But the report of this feast mentions only roasted meats, presumes quality breads and choice wines. Nothing would be too much for this feast. But serving this quality of food to peasants is almost as foolish as feeding it to swine. Finally, nobody did anything for another person without expecting some return. Charity begins at home, but if someone feeds the hungry, clothes the naked, etc. and does so with no expectation of return, this would be utter folly (which is why the behavior of the "Good Samaritan" is so foolish). Will this king get anything in return for making people eat his feast?

108

What is wrong with this picture? A king bringing riff-raff to his table? This is so laughable! A powerful monarch reduced to this?! But no king in the audience's ken would act so foolishly. Peasants treated with dignity? Hilarious! Jesus grabs their attention with this preposterous story of a king feeding the least and lowliest at his banquet. He seems, moreover, pressured to do something a king would never do. What a foolish king! Thus, at every step in the story, the peasant audience laughs. It gets crazier and they laugh more loudly. Everything is exaggerated, impossible and over-the-top. The only proper response is to laugh with contempt at the king.

But Jesus abruptly stops speaking; now the audience gets the message that laughter is no longer appropriate. In their surprise they does not know what to he is doing or how to respond. From noise to silence! Unsure silence. By shutting up, Jesus still communicates, but now the audience has to listen hard to what is being said by this "silence." What are they to make of so foolish as king as one who would feed a banquet to peasant no-bodies? What to make of this foolish king? As the silence settles in, hearers are forced to shift from hearing a story that made them laugh to imagining that the story was a puzzle, a problem to be solved, an exercise in imaginative play, beyond entertaining laughter. They gradually—at least the clever ones—catch on to Jesus' new calculus: foolish is wise; least are greatest. Think "honor and shame." But who is shamed? Who is honored? And why? Does anyone care? Read Jesus's face: what does he look like when he shuts up? Can you see anyone in the audience getting the puzzle or the riddle? But once this audience gets used to Jesus' funny stories, they might compare them and ask what is common to them? Does Jesus have a preferred way of telling funny stories? Do they overlap in meaning? Does the solution to one aid in solving the riddle in others?

Laughing at the Landlord (Mark 12:1–12)

Much in this story would be familiar to peasant farmers. Agriculture: a vineyard; landless tenants forced to earn a living by tending another's land; absentee landlords who live in luxury in the cities (Matt 21:33–46; Luke 12:33–40; 16:1–8), servants of the landlord who do his bidding, even to the point of abusing other servants (Mark 13:34–36; Luke 12:36–47). Peasants know of fields with fences to protect prize crops; they know of the investment made by the landlord to have a first-class vineyard. At harvest time, the absentee landlord begins to bring the harvest from his farm into the city to support him and his elite peers for the rest of the year. So far, all is as it should be. Nothing funny here.

Although by contract the landlord is owed "his share of the produce of the vineyard," the tenants rebel and beat three bands of slaves whom the master successively sends to collect his share of the harvest. No more "same old same old"! Peasants would now side with the tenants against the landlord, for either they or some of their kin regularly suffer at the hands of the rich. Moreover, the "tenant farmers" are most likely victims of debt foreclose, who would have sympathizers in the crowd listening. Thus, the audience laughs at the comeuppance of the landlord; for once the tenants are not the victims of the elite. All fantasy, however. If there is laughter, it is directed at the absentee landlord. The audience, however, are certain that the rich landowner must seek vengeance for the insults he has suffered. While peasants would laugh at the humiliation of this landlord, eventually the old order must be re-established; blood must flow; shame avenged. This is the way of the world. So we hear fragile laughter.

While it lasts, the story is typically one of exaggeration, over-the-top and hyperbole. Why? 1. Everyone knows that the landlord does not act like an honor-sensitive elite who should strike back quickly to restore his standing with his tenant farmers. 2. How foolish not to round up a posse and ride out for revenge. Strange! Foolish! Shameful! 3. His foolishness is public: not only are his own slaves confound, but his peers become angry with him for letting a peasants' revolt get started. No self-respecting landlord would ever let rebellious tenants get away with this behavior! Yet, this is the stuff of laughter, guffawing, etc. 4. With all of the audiences' sympathy flowing toward the tenants, they savor the embarrassment of the landlord and laugh at his ineptitude. 5. You thought it could not get zanier? The owner sits and ponders. "He had still one other, a beloved son." Finally he sent this son to them, saying, "They will respect my son."

We imagine the peasants in Jesus' audience become hysterical with laughter at the final solution of the landlord to send his "beloved" son, his heir, to persuade thieves and murderers. This, gentle reader, is clearly over-the-top foolishness. Has the audience ever heard of anything so foolish, so stupid, so shameful. Everything is wrong with this picture! The audience should laugh. By now, the old world has been turned upside down: rebelling tenants prevail while the owner seems powerless. The weak seem to have put down the strong (Luke 1:51–53). This not how the world works when peasants disrespect the owner of the vineyard. Clever audiences know that the actual parable ends with the sending of the son, but not at the head of an army. All the rest of the story is the domestication of the story to bring it into conformity with the old, predictable order. The rich and strong always prevail. This is by no means part of Jesus' story.

But true to form, after narrating that the son is sent, Jesus goes silent. All laughter dies. What was Jesus trying to tell them? Not just entertainment, surely? Now it's riddle time: who is this absentee landlord? The folly of the story might be precisely the point. Can such folly actually be wisdom? Can Jesus be praising this? Do Jesus's eyes give a "tell" as to what he is thinking? Does this absentee landlord share anything in common with the foolish king? Or other protagonists of other parables? Does it help if we remember how often Jesus prefaced his parables with "The Kingdom of heaven is like . . ." (Matt 13:24, 31, 33)? Now is the time to study Jesus's face: what is he saying by his silence?

The Foolish King and the Enormous Debt (Matt 18:23–27)

When trying to make an imaginative scenario of this very small parable, we need to know more about the precarious life of a typical peasant. "Debt" is a nasty four-letter word to them. It seems that most of them borrowed heavily to pay this year's taxes. They know, alas, that loans must be repaid, and so they live uneasily all the time. Without repayment, the land will default the lenders. This is scary business. So an accurate scenario would imagine 50-100 debtors lined up outside the dwelling of the king, waiting to repay their debt. Hence, at the opening of the story, everything is as it should be: nothing is wrong with this picture, not even the determination of the king to sell a debtor and his family into slavery to pay off the debt. If he does not foreclose, he will lose face and respect, and be taken for a fool, a patsy, a soft touch. We typically have debts to pay for our houses, cars, various loans, etc. But we have jobs and salaries with which to pay these debts back. But this was not the case for Jesus' audience.

Cameo 25: Jesus's Intimate Acquaintance and Concern with Debt
Material from the earliest Jesus traditions records the following concern for debt:
1. allusions to debtor's prison (Luke 12:58–59/Matt 5:25–26; 2. the story of the Un-
forgiving Servant (Matt 18:23–35); 3. the parable of the Two Debtors (Luke 7:41–
42; and 4. the Widow's copper coin (Mark 12:41–44). The parables of the Talents
(Luke 19:12–27/Matt 25:14–30) and the Unjust Steward (Luke 16:1–8) describe the
oppressiveness of the "thief" and creditor.

So we would try to imagine Jesus' peasant world and the constant pressure to pay debts, which was generally not possible. Into this swamp, the
narrative suddenly becomes hyperbolic and unimaginable. The king does
in fact respond with compassion to a debtor's plight—the first time such a
thing has ever been heard of. "Out of pity for him, the lord of that slave released him and forgave him the debt" (Matt 18:27). Crazy, no? Outrageous
behavior! This is not real! Moreover, the king acts with consummate folly
by cancelling the debt. Lenders never show sympathy to the borrowers.
Loans must always be repaid; debts are cancelled only in dreams. But this
is what the king does. He changes from utmost severity to utmost folly by
cancelling the debt. The reaction of the audience? Laughter! Laughter at the
king's foolishness, because all will think him silly, weak and shameful. This
has never happened in their memory; the story, moreover, makes the bad
guy look good. Did they shout "boo!" or "bravo" at the King's actions. Since
the behavior of this mighty man is over-the-top and hyperbolic, laughter
would be the appropriate reaction. "Not in your dreams."

This must be considered a genuine parable. 1. The audience immediately knows the situation; 2. the protagonist, the King, starts out acting
normally, acting according to the accepted norm of justice; 3. but quickly
he becomes laughable when "out of pity," the lord of that slave forgave him
the debt; 4. this action is utterly laughable because it is so unusual, over the
top and foolish; 5. by this he turns the world upside down by canceling the
debt. The world doesn't and cannot operate this way. And so, when Jesus
stopped speaking, his hearers stopped laughing. What he told them in the
parable is laughable, but by his silence Jesus signals that the funny story has
become a riddle.

Are there any clues that the audience can use to solve this riddle? A
couple can be found in Matt 18, such as Peter's question about just how
many sins should be forgiven; Jesus' answer may apply here (Matt 18:21–
22). And in another place Jesus said: "It is not the will of your Father in

heaven that one of these little ones should be lost" (Matt 18:14). So if a disciple remembers how Jesus often sat in the midst of tax collectors and sinners, they may see the connection to the cancelling of debts here.

Not All Thieves Are in Jail (Luke 19:11–27)

Just as a stupid farmer achieved 30, 60, 100% increase in harvest, and the man who owed 10,000 talents received debt remission, so too in this parable incredible sums of money are treated casually, as if they were part of the landscape, but are really the stuff of fantasy. Remember that very poor peasants are listening to this; and Jesus is not lecturing on economics. What do they know that we don't? They know how preposterously large 5 talents are; they know that there is no legitimate way to get the increase that the clients got; and they can't imagine anyone being rewarded with "cities." They can only think that the master must be some big-time person who himself can amass such wealth. They also know how typically parables and stories feature an absent master, whose return is sure but uncertain (Matt 12:36; 18:23; Luke 16:2). Moreover, when the master returns, he will demand an accounting, another regular feature in the parables. Furthermore, they know the burden of taxes, how they were collected and where their taxes went. We imagine that peasants could distinguish tax collectors from thieves only with difficulty We will need this "high context" information shortly. What scenario would the audience imagine in that "high context" world when they hear about these large sums and about the description of the master in 18:24–25? How do they think about taxes and tax collectors?

Cameo 26: Tax Collectors, Taxes, and Debt

Tax collectors, taxes, and tithes are regular features of Jesus's landscape. He himself pays the Temple tax (Matt 17:24–27) and "gives to Caesar . . ." (Mark 12:14–17). Every Israelites paid some monarch a "head tax" and a "land tax," often very steep. Note the unusual generosity of Demetrius to Israel: "I free you and exempt all the Jews from payment of tribute and salt tax and crown levies, and instead of collecting the third of the grain and the half of the fruit of the trees that I should receive, I release them from this day" (1 Macc 10:29–31). Now reverse this and imagine what they regularly paid. Israelites, moreover, pay tithes.

Tax/Toll Collectors: Caesar auctioned off the right to collect taxes to rich and powerful men: "The prominent men purchased the right to farm the taxes in their several provinces and collect the sum fixed" (Josephus, *Antiquities* 12.154–155). Anything in excess went into the tax collector's pocket, e.g., Zacchaeus, a chief tax collector, was very wealthy (Luke 19:2–9). Absent landlords, such as Caesar, Herod, Jerusalem elites and local elites, owned most of the (good) land, and peasants generally small plots. The former paid no taxes, only the latter. Taxation, which could be up to 40% of a crop, forced many to borrow, go into debt, and then lose their land. Everyone knows this. Can you imagine the wealth an energetic tax collector could gather?

When we attempt to make an imaginative scenario of this, our attention at first centers of the three client to whom the wealth is distributed. Our major question is to guess if all three clients will succeed; and if not, which ones will and which ones won't. The first two take their wealth and make an impossible profit with it, profit unimaginable in the real world, much less in that of the peasants. One increases the master's wealth five fold, and the other two fold. The audience knows that the only way to increase wealth so dramatically is to take the wealth from others, as soldiers do when they take spoils. Commerce won't do it. Military means? But nothing in the story suggests that they are military chiefs. Yet another way to great wealth comes from being one of the chief tax collectors. Remember that Zacchaeus was "a chief tax-collector and was rich" (Luke 19:2). It matters if the great increase in wealth was gained as spoils or by taxation. This will determine how the audience evaluates the first two clients of the master. Keep imagining this as another of Jesus' puzzling parables.

How would the audience of Jesus react to this part of the story? Laughter, surely, because everything described is over the top, excessive, hyperbolic: the sums intrusted, their amazing increase and the preposterous rewards. Such hyperbole always brings laughter—not approval, but laughter. The more outrageous the sums involved, the louder the audience's laughter. Since the master praises the actions of the first two, his positive reaction to them endorses the laughter of the audience. Moreover, the master treats each client with exceptional honor: "Well done, good servant! Because you have been trustworthy in *a very small thing* (oh, really?), take charge of *ten cities*." "The second came, saying, 'Lord, your two pounds has made five pounds.' He said to him, 'And you, rule over *five cities*'" (Luke 19:17–19). "Cities," no less; it appears that the two clients of the master have become petty rulers over their own kingdoms (please check Matt 19:28). Jesus's audience probably laughs at the hyperbole of this story: so much wealth, too much profit, outrageous rewards. But, honestly, this is the way the world works. No surprises here.

How, then, would they react to the third client? After all, he did the culturally honorable thing and did NOT risk shaming the master by losing the money. But we have to assess him in terms of the way the parable unfolds and in terms of that world. What we personally think of him must be put aside. Only when he and his master come face-to-face can we see what is really going on. First, he admits, "Lord, here is your pound. I wrapped it up in a piece of cloth." This puts his behavior in stark contrast to that of the other two clients; both cannot be right. If they had the master's favor, what can this man expect? But, why did this third man do this? Not because of some law or moral principle! No, "*I was afraid of you,* because you are a harsh man; you take what you did not deposit, and reap what you did not sow" (19:22).

Now it is out in the open; the "harsh" master is unquestionably a *thief*, who else does this: "you take what you did not deposit, and reap what you did not sow." He is a thief, and a chief of thieves. But what does this insight mean? This third client has known all along that his master is "a harsh man" which "harshness" relates mainly to his behavior as a thief: "You take what you did not deposit, and reap what you did not sow." Click! This suggests that the *source* of all the wealth in the story is *the same for all characters in the story*: the master, the first two clients, and the third one (after all, the master gave him 1 talent, i.e., "stolen property"). Did peasants regularly encounter thieves? No, but experienced the expropriation of their harvest. In that culture we would be right to imagine that "theft" = "taxes," certainly in peasant eyes.

But what is the appropriate reaction here? What sort of background is needed to appreciate what this third client has done. According to the story, his folly lies in his *refusal to continue doing what he always did*. How did he get the master's attention in the first place? What did the master think of him to entrust him with the enormous sum of one talent? He was once part of the group; his behavior was like that of the others, only on a much lower scale. So he, too, was a thief. His folly apparently lay in the fact that he *stopped playing the same game* as did the others. He no longer *imitated his master*. So, imitating the master is the key to success and praise, which in this case means being a thief in imitation of the master. And this is the way to praise and reward. Thus, the wise and good thing is to imitate the master. Yes, "thieves" here are declared honorable. So, the proper reaction to the third man would be laughter at his folly. What a foolish thing to do! How can you be so dumb? He could be rich and powerful. If the audience clapped for the first two clients, they boo here. So, our evaluation of the third man rests on his contrast with the two who were praised and his acknowledgment that his master is a "thief" and he was one too. The master honored them because they followed him acutely, but he has only contempt for the third man because he stopped being a disciple or imitator of the master.

Keep remembering that in a typical parable the world gets turned topsy-turvy. So if the first two clients did the "right" thing, then the last one did the "wrong" thing." Of course this does not have to do with the morality of "theft," because in the logic of parables, when the world is turned upside down, last becomes first, least is greatest, and folly is wisdom. Here "theft" is praised and rewarded. What a crazy world! So the audience is not shocked at the revelation that the master is the chief of thieves; the shock comes when one asks why the third client quit. As the story goes, he is a fool and his refusal to play the game is considered zany enough that he is expelled from the team. The audience would laugh at his folly. How can anyone be so dumb, so insane, so blind.

But the only figure in the story who truly matters, the protagonist, is indisputably a thief. Does Jesus want us to mock him and laugh at him? On the one hand, he is only doing "what comes naturally"—for a thief, that is. Thieves, of course, are ok, as long as they are robbing someone else or robbing the rich. If they were robbing the nobles and royals, the audience would laugh until it hurt. It is probably an anachronism to imagine the master as an early version of Robin Hood. In the conflict between the powerful rich and bandits, Jesus' peasant audience would root for the bandits. So, let's focus on this main character in the story who moves the plot along.

How does Jesus imagine this figure? Yes, he is a thief of great magnitude, but are we sure that we know how the audience would consider this thief or any thief? How do we know that "thief" automatically suggests sin and evil? ("Thou shalt not steal.") But might "thief" be understood paradoxically? Does it help if you remember how often Jesus himself was referred to as a thief; obviously those authors imagined it paradoxically. Several times in Revelation the Jesus figure publicly declares: "If you do not wake up, I will come like a thief" (3:3) and "See, I am coming like a thief" (16:15). The day of the Lord was often likened to the arrival of a thief: "The day of the Lord will come like a thief in the night." (1 Thess 5:2; 2 Pet 3:10). How many times did Jesus tell his disciples to "stay awake," to be ready for the thief who comes when least expected" (Luke 12:28; Mark 13:34). While we abhor thieves, in their culture "thieves" could play different roles and so be imagined as good or bad. If a parable is supposed to turn the world upside-down, then all of the ingredients are here. A "thief" might be doing the right or honorable thing. His co-thieves are honorable because they imitate the master. In a topsy-turvy world, this is not hard to imagine.

Jesus never tells us how he evaluates the Chief Thief, but he implies it. The time comes when Jesus goes silent. Although the gospels often note that the dumbfounded disciples ask for an explanation, that is not the case here. At a certain point, he stops talking and looks at them as if to say, "Now, your turn!" Chew on this!" You wrestle with this riddle. Remember, Jesus was always saying "the Kingdom of Heaven is like . . ." How do we put together "thief" and "kingdom of God? Any clues, Jesus? Go back to certain stories where foolish farmers and zany landlords become heroes. These are the very folk that peasants would love to see get their comeuppance, but whom Jesus seems to praise. What could a first-class thief have in common with a king and a landlord?

"Who Is My Neighbor?" (Luke 10:29–37)

Yes, this is a parable, but here it functions as a specific answer to a pointed question. When we read it, we can't help imagine it as a nasty response to a hostile attack. In its present context it serves to embarrass the questioner. Jesus has just taught that the core of the Law is love of God and *love of neighbor*; but then his interlocutor attacks him, "testing" him with a question: "Who is my neighbor?" Usually Jesus answers a hostile question with his own question, as he eventually does later: "Which of these three was a neighbor to the man who fell victim to the robbers?" (10:36). But, while the parable is used to silence an enemy, it is a genuine parable which should be looked at independent of Luke's use of it.

It helps to imagine that Jesus' peasant audience would have strong feelings about the characters and events in the story, unknown to modern listeners. In a native's imaginative scenario, robbers are ubiquitous, so the victim was a fool to go alone on a dangerous journey – no sympathy here, only laughter for he got what he deserved. But the "priest" and "Levite," who by-pass the victim, are also laughed at; for the are the elite, the high and mighty ones, whose "purity concerns" trump common expectation of help for a victim, which, unfortunately, is no surprise to the peasants. The wounded man is not kin, so they have no obligation to help. Peasants know, moreover, that such people demand a tithe of all that they, the peasants, produce, just for being priests and Levites. Laughter is appropriate because the stereotype of such people is dramatized here. They are too busy with the things of God to help a fellow Israelite, yet this is predictable behavior for them.

Along comes the most unlikely person to give aid: a Samaritan – not even an Israelite, but an apostate—and a merchant to boot. He certainly is not kin to the wounded man, for he is of a tribe and place which is hostile to Israel (see John 4:9; Luke 9:52). He is held in contempt by peasants because all know that merchants are thieves: they buy cheap and sell dear; that is, merchants always live at the expense of the buyer. This merchant's animal carried "wine and oil," traditional trade goods, which he buys cheap and sells dear. But, to the audience's shock, the merchant stops, expends some of his wears on the victim's wounds, sits him on his own animal, and takes him to lodging—*all without thought of recompense*. Loud laughter at this very foolish behavior. This peasant audience considers the man a fool who does very foolish things. Moreover, this foolish merchant gives the innkeeper what we call a "blank check," a promise to make good on all extra expenses for the victim on his return: "Take care of him; and when I come back, I will repay you whatever more you spend" (Luke 10:35). Barter, all know, is the norm: you give and you get, which is also the norm for settling disputes ("an eye for an eye . . ."). But this Samaritan, presumably a "thief" in peasants' eyes, gives outright and seeks no barter or exchange in return.

How exceptionally rare this is in peasant's eyes where everything is scarce, and everything proffered is a loan to be repaid. "Lending" was so unusual that Jesus had to command it: "Lend to those in need" (Luke 6:34). The audience, therefore, is justified at laughing at this behavior, which is over the top, foolish, and unimaginable.

What's wrong with this picture? In a "high context" culture, everything! Ethnic comrades might be expected to aid one of their own, but they don't. An outsider, considered an apostate and a thief, acts foolishly to "give and not get." The norm is no longer "give and get," but "give without expectation of return." Is Jesus kidding? Can he be saying this? If "charity begins at home," this merchant is all the more a fool to be laughed at. He acts in folly, and lets himself be taken advantage of. This foolish behavior turns the world upside down. He is another of the zany protagonists who people the parables and give the audience a good laugh.

When Jesus went silent, the audience was faced with a riddle to be solved. How to assess the behavior of the Samaritan? Everything is wrong with his actions, yet they seem to be approved, at least in the language of parables. But Jesus cuts the laughter short when he turns to the man who asked the hostile question, which provoked this story. "'Who was neighbor to the man in need?' 'The one who showed him mercy'" (Luke 10:36-37). Thus Jesus is himself telling us how to evaluate the story and how to imagine the behavior of the Samaritan. This completely takes the story out of the realm of parables and turns it into a teaching. But what would the original audience think who were not told this final part of the story? Most likely in the original telling of this parable, Luke 10:25, ended the story. Jesus then became silent and let his disciple wrestle with this riddle.

With the question to the lawyer, the story which made the peasants laugh is no longer funny; seriousness prevails. Jesus has silenced his enemy, a cause for cheering, and in doing so turns the riddle into a teaching, to which laughter is inappropriate. In a final touch of irony, Jesus makes his opponent tell him the proper understanding of the story; the one who was "neighbor" to the wounded man is the hero, no matter how foolish he appeared: "the one who showed him mercy." So, as an audience imagines this parable, they would realize how intrusive of the real parable the exhortation in 10:36 actually is. They know that the upside down world has been turned back in place. Far from being a story about a foolish protagonist, it becomes an exhortation to commonplace behavior. It clearly illustrates "love your neighbor."

But going back to the original parable, when Jesus went silent he turned the parable into a riddle. His audience would stop laughing at the Samaritan. What is this all about? Who is the protagonist? The solution lies in comparing this foolish protagonist with other foolish figures in other parables. They all have something in common for "those who have ears to hear." When Jesus shut up, he turned a funny story into a riddle or puzzle. All along laughter was an appropriate response, that is, until Jesus went silent. Now they must confront the riddle. What they thought was worthy of laughter is put on hold. They have to decide what to think about this "foolish" Samaritan?

A World Truly Turned Upside Down (Matt 25:31–46)

The pastoral scenario described in this parable, while very familiar to Jesus' audience, has scant place in our imagination. Our default scenario for sheep and goats is the children's part of the zoo; but Jesus' audience imagined them grazing on hillsides, protected by a shepherd. In a gender-divided world, sheep belong to the male world, because only a man or boy was allowed out in the open to pasture them. A goat, however, is an animal allied with females: it did not stray from home, and so need no pasture; its value lay primarily in the milk it produced. It had value, but nothing like that of a sheep.

Both animals have a "cultural history" as well. Sheep are considered affectionate and non-aggressive (2 Sam 12:3; Isa 53:7), as well as defenseless (Mic 5:8), whereas goats are aggressive, temperamental, and destructive. Sheep are silent when shorn or sacrificed, not so goats; sheep, moreover, require constant care and supervision, whereas goats do not (Num 27:17; 2 Sam 12:3). This last item may help us distinguish sheep from goats in Matt 25. Sheep require constant care, a summary of which Ezekiel provides:

> I will rescue them from all the places to which they have been scat-
> tered . . . I will bring them out . . . bring them into their own land; and I
> will feed them on the mountains of Israel, by the watercourses, and in
> all the inhabited parts of the land. I will feed them with good pasture;
> they shall lie down in good grazing land, and they shall feed on rich
> pasture. (Ezek 34:12–14)

Goats can survive on scraps from the household. Since each animal has a distinctive reputation, the audience appreciates the contrasting behaviors of their shepherds, which correlate with being either on the "left," a sinister location, or on the "right," always a favorable position.

While interesting, the animals are not the focus of the story. Rather, the contrasting behaviors of those who tended each animal becomes the central focus of the parables, which behavior all judge according to common norms known and accepted. The King addresses the shepherds of the sheep first. He calls them "Honorable." But why? "'Come, you that are blessed by my Father, inherit the kingdom prepared for you from the foundation of the world" (25:34). Amazing, but what have they done to deserve such an honorable reward? The King then lists their deeds: "For I was hungry and you gave me food, I was thirsty and you gave me something to drink, I was a stranger and you welcomed me, was naked and you gave me clothing, etc." (25:35–36). Peasants hearing would begin to laugh at the behavior of these shepherds, because it is foolish to give and not get something in return, which is what these shepherds did. "Reciprocity" served as the norm in "high culture" scenario, which means that is foolish to give to another with no expectation of a return. All in the story, shepherds of both the sheep and the goats, know this common knowledge, as well as Jesus' audience. Peasant shepherds simply cannot do this because it exhausts their own resources. Yet there is another thing wrong with this picture. It matters greatly whether those in need who come to these shepherds are kin to them? There is an expectation in justice to support one's family; but these beggars have no claim to the attention and concern of these shepherds. Two major problems, then, are presented by the parable.

At this point the audience, who know all too well how the world works, realize that this parable contradicts what they know. Hence the behavior of the shepherds of the sheep in their eyes is strange indeed, foolish, ridiculous, and so deserves laughter. What we approve of, they considered foolish. We lack important information about the world of the audience to appreciate just how foolish this behavior is. When they hear "hungry and you fed me, naked and you clothed me" (25:35–36), they laugh at the foolish behavior of these shepherds and the equally foolish behavior of the King. How can anything so foolish be called "Honorable"? Therefore, they consider this behavior so radical that it turns their world upside down. Their world simply does not work like the narrative of this parable. To appreciate the problem before the audience, we need the basic structure of barter and exchange to form a valid scenario of the problem.

Cameo 27: Does Charity Begin at Home?

All in the that world understood that there were three forms of exchange. 1. *Generalized* reciprocity, which describes altruistic attention to the wants and needs of another. It characterizes kinship and hospitality ("charity begins at home"). 2. *Balanced* reciprocity, which considers the mutual interests of both parties in a symmetrical way (i.e., give and get; quid pro quo). This constitutes the typical communication between neighbors, namely, trade agreements, fees payed for services and barter. 3. *Negative* reciprocity seeks self-interest at the expense a stranger or enemy. It calculates how to get maximum profit, while giving as little as possible in return. Comparisons may tease out the important differences.

GENERALIZED reciprocity: 1. *characteristic*: give without expectation of return; 2. *forms*: child rearing, caring for parents, hospitality; 3. *recipients*: parents, children, kin; 4. *biblical examples*: Matt 7:11/Luke 11:11–13; Luke 10:33-35.

BALANCED reciprocity: 1. *characteristic*: tit-for-tat, quid-pro-quo; 2. *forms*: barter, assistance agreements; 3. *recipients*: neighbors; 4. *biblical examples*: 1 Cor 9:3–12; Matt 10:10/Luke 10:7

NEGATIVE reciprocity: 1. *characteristic*: get and don't give; 2. *forms*: theft, taxes, and merchant exchange; 3. *recipients*: people with whom one does not live, enemies, strangers; 4. *biblical examples*: see parable of the "thief" above.

At this point the audience knows all too well how the world works. Hence the behavior of the shepherds of the sheep in their eyes is strange, foolish, ridiculous, and so deserves laughter. They know that in this case, since "charity begins at home," just how foolish these shepherds are. They laugh at the excessive generosity shown the no-bodies who come to the shepherds. Their world, therefore, operates on the principle of "balanced" reciprocity: they give and they get; they lend and receive back. But to the great surprise of all, the King tells them something more preposterous when he declares that each of the beggars supported by the shepherds was actually the *King himself*, but in disguise. They didn't and couldn't see that they were (foolishly) giving to the King. So they express amazement: "And when was it that we saw you as stranger and welcomed you, or naked and gave you clothing? And when was it that we saw you sick or in prison and visited you?" The King answers them, "Just as you did it to one of the least of these *who are members of my family*, you did it to me." If the world was turned upside down when the King called their foolish behavior "honorable," this completes the conversion of their balanced world into a topsy-turvy one.

How radical is the information of the King in the hearing of all characters, the shepherds and the audience. What they evaluated as foolish is wise and virtuous. It takes such a King to turn their world upside down when he calls honorable what they thought of as foolish. This, however, is both funny and scary: funny, because they cannot imagine a king masquerading as a beggar; and scary because things are not what they seem. In this case, the foolish did the wise thing, even though they did not know it. And so, their actions of feeding the hungry, giving water to the thirsty, welcoming the stranger, etc. were virtuous, worthy of praise in the eyes of the King. Everybody in the story, except for the King, evaluated the shepherds' behavior as foolish, hardly worth of praise and reward. Their world as been completely turned upside down and topsy turvy. The King has the last word.

What about the shepherds of the goats on the left? They had a good laugh at the foolishness of the sheep's shepherds, foolishness which deserves laugher. But they are immediately silenced and stunned. In their eyes and in the hearing of Jesus' these shepherds did the right thing, which does not deserve laughter. Nevertheless, they are banished from the King's presence because they did not do the actions which the King has just praised. This shakes the audience like an earthquake. In peasants' eyes they acted prudently and appropriately. For them, "charity did began at home." and justice directed them to pay their dues to those to whom they were obligated (i.e., kin). They followed common sense, and they were prudent. The shepherds of the sheep should be laughed at by their neighbors, but not the shepherds of the goats. But the King turns the world upside down and topsy turvy. The "foolish" shepherds of the sheep are praised and the honorable shepherds of the, goats are shamed. The king is turning the world upside down and topsy turvy, because in his eyes, those who were imprudent and foolish in fact did the just and wise thing. But those who thought they were acting prudently (an in accord with village norms) are exposed as acting in error, a mistake so serious as to cause their downfall.

How can this be? In the world of Jesus' parables we often find such an overturning of conventional values and behavior. And this is just one more example. "Let those who have ears and *remember* . . ."

Given the great shock of a world turning upside down, are there any clues for those hearing the parable. If the audience remembers how virtuous it was in Jesus' eyes to give a cup of water (Mark 9:41; Matt 10:42) or "Give to everyone who begs from you, and do not refuse anyone who wants to borrow from you" (Matt 5:42), that person might well figure out this riddle. And if a disciple remembered how many times Jesus declared a value system topsy-turvy, they might bring that to bear on this story. Remember:

1. Last is first/first is last
   (Matt 19:30; 20:16; Mark 9:35; 10:31; Luke 13:30)

2. Smallest is greatest/greatest is smallest
   (Matt 13:32; Mark 4:32; see Luke 7:28)

3. Humbled is exalted/exalted is humbled
   (Matt 23:12; Luke 14:11; 18:14)

4. Losing is saving/saving is losing
   (Matt 10:39; 16:25; Mark 8:35; Luke 9:24; 17:33).

Thus, a disciple with ears to hear might imagine how this parable compares with other of Jesus' stories.

8

Imagining Jesus at Prayer

In this final contemplation of Jesus in his own culture, we seek to imagine him praying. That is, since he is often recorded as "praying," who taught him to pray? what prayers was he taught? what sort of faith development could there be from a toddler to an adolescent to an "elder"? Continuing the thesis of this book, we suggest that Jesus was *taught* through his entire life to know God, to worship God, to petition and praise God, and other acts of piety common to Israelites of his time. *He was taught all of this. He had to learn all of this*, just as all Israelites in his world were taught and learned to be observant members of the covenant. As we saw in the front of this book, "He worked with human hands, he thought with a human mind. He acted with a human will, and with a human heart he loved" (*Gaudium et Spes* #22). Put simply, he learned with his human mind and will and heart to acknowledge and honor God as he was taught by family and peers.

Before all else, we need to know how Jesus and contemporaries understood human growth and development, that is, how they broke a life into various stages and talked about what was common in each stage. This type of thinking clearly understood that humans developed and grew in wisdom and grace. The most common assessment of life-stages listed only three: "youth . . . prime of life . . . and old age." This scheme is found in Aristotle and in 1 John 2:12–14. Pythagoras used the four seasons of the year to map a man's life-span: "Twenty years a boy, twenty years a youth, twenty years a young man, twenty years an old man; and these four periods correspond to the four seasons, the boy to spring, the youth to summer, the young man to autumn, and the old man to winter," meaning by youth one not yet grown up and by a young man a man of mature age" (Diogenes Laertius 8.10). Finally, some of the ancients talked about ten stages of development which chronicle both physical and mental development. Philo lists seven, following the pattern of Solon (*Creation* 103–105). Since the development of Jesus from infancy to old age is so important for this consideration, we cite Philo:

> The perfecting power of the number seven is shown by the stages of men's growth, measured from infancy to old age in the following manner: during the first period of seven years the growth of the teeth begins; during the second the capacity for emitting seed; in the third the growing of the beard; in the fourth increase of strength; in the fifth again ripeness for marriage; in the sixth the understanding reaches its bloom; in the seventh progressive improvement and development of mind and reason; in the eighth the perfecting of both these; during the ninth forbearance and gentleness emerge, owing to the more complete taming of the passions; during the tenth comes the desirable end of life, while the bodily organs are still compact and firm.

Philo himself chronicles ten life-stages based on the model of Solon, indicating a "high context" understanding. The point of this should be obvious: each human being grows through clearly defined states of development. The boy is not the youth is not the adult is not the elder. This corresponds with both physical maturation and intellectual acuity. Thus the prayer of a boy will correspond to his capacities, and the same with the other stages. This necessarily means that a boy-youth-man such as Jesus grew and developed; his body was never the same at each stage, nor was his mind and spirit. While "nature" takes care of the body by food and exercise, the mind needed to be taught everything it came to know. This especially means the faith of Jesus at various stages.

Each gospel describes Jesus in various ways, according to the context of the particular group to whom it was addressed, that is, each gospel was contextual, in and of itself. But while they all talk about Jesus, explicitly telling us something about Jesus' training, they simply presume most things— namely, what "high context" presumes that all in that cultural would know. For example, consider the socialization of Jesus to be an observant Israelite, as reconstructed from fragmentary references.

Only Luke's Gospel states that Jesus was circumcised on the eighth day, on which day he was named (Luke 2:21), and was dedicated to God as the first-born male forty days later (Luke 2:22–23). But everyone knew that all males were circumcised as a sign of belonging to the covenant. Only Luke states that: "Every year his parents went to Jerusalem for the festival of the Passover. And when he was twelve years old, they went up as usual for the festival" (2:41–42). Of course he continued to celebrate Passover at the appropriate time, either back in Jerusalem or in Nazareth. It is assumed that observant Israelites celebrated Passover annually in the traditional manner, and we assume that Jesus did so. Only John's narrative informs us that Jesus went on pilgrimage to Jerusalem to celebrate the "Feast of Booths" (John 7:8—8:59) and "Dedication" (John 10:22–42). These feasts need not be celebrated in Jerusalem; Nazareth was good enough. Besides this annual calendar of feasts, Jesus also attended the synagogue every Sabbath ("as was his custom," Luke 4:16), at least from the time when he was disciplined enough to honor the males who trained him in proper male behavior. We can only guess at the many circumcisions, weddings, funerals, etc., Jesus attended over his lifetime, all of which would reinforce his appreciation of the proper ways of celebrating according to the traditions found in the Scriptures. It is up to the imagination of someone trying to create an accurate imaginative scenario to fill this new house with furniture brought from earlier parts of this book.

All current readers were once toddlers, children, adolescents, etc. who were taught by their parents (as well as in schools or CCD programs) how to pray and how to be Christian. Moreover, most of the readers of this book have raised their own children, and so know first-hand the extended process of socializing a child into faith. Although we cannot recall all that happened to socialize us as observant and reverent Christians, we know with certainty that we experienced a socializing process. And we have first-hand experience of trying to socialize our own children to be believers. We already know much of the structure of being taught and teaching others the "faith of our fathers (and mothers)," so, even if all details cannot be historically proven, we know of a process which took years and which included group teaching by family, Sunday School, and parish prayer, etc. Put simply, *we were all taught everything we came to know and we all learned about God and Jesus only through being taught.* Let us bring that experience into the process of contemplating Jesus being taught and learning how to pray.

When we present the teaching and learning of Jesus according to the events and feasts we are sure Jesus celebrated (hence, learned), we necessarily begin with the traditional prayers that all Israelites prayed: once a day, twice a day, weekly, etc. These are the most likely places where socialization would occur.

Contemplation 1: Watching Jesus Praying

We have a good idea of what took place in *a typical synagogue service*: prayers of praise and petition, readings from the Torah, and perhaps a homily. Of course psalms were recited and stories from the Torah were narrated, so that a young boy could readily learn the narrative of the House of Israel, as well as ways of prayer and worship by sheer repetition of the materials. We know that this service happened weekly, the likely nursery of Jesus' learning to pray, when he was old enough to attend. But the adult Jesus also learned along the way adult prayers and practices, especially "blessings."

The gospels themselves state again and again that Jesus *"blessed"* bread, at ordinary and festival meals, as well as on open hillsides and sea shores. I think that the ritual of blessing bread by Jesus was, if not identical, then very similar to the traditional one: "Blessed are You, Lord our God, King of the universe, Who brings forth bread from the earth." The blessing would be spoken at every meal. Its infinite repetition engraved it in a boy's or an adult's memory.

It is rather surprising to find so few mentions of Jesus "praying" in the gospels (that is, an action described by use of the words "pray/prayer"). Again, this is something presumed by writers writing in a "high context" environment. Here are the few places where Jesus is actually described by the use of the words "pray" and "prayer."

> **Cameo 28: Miscellaneous Remarks about Jesus "Praying"**
>
> "Then little children were being brought to him in order that he might *lay his hands on them and pray.*" (Matt 19:13)
>
> "In the morning, while it was still very dark, he got up and went out to a deserted place, and there he prayed." (Mark 1:35)
>
> "After saying farewell, he went up on the mountain to pray . . ." (Mark 6:46)
>
> "But he would withdraw to deserted places and pray . . ." (Luke 5:16)
>
> "Now during those days he went out to the mountain to pray; and he spent the night in prayer to God." (Luke 6:12)
>
> "Jesus took with him Peter, John and James, and went up on the mountain to pray." (Luke 9:28)
>
> "He was praying in a certain place, and after he had finished . . ." (Luke 11:1)
>
> "But I have prayed for you that your own faith may not fail . . ." (Luke 22:32)
>
> *Some easy patterns emerge*: 1. *Where?* Jesus prays on mountains, occasionally at a "certain" place, often in a "deserted" place. 2. *When?* he prays before sunrise, at night, and any time convenient; 3. *Posture?*: he regularly stands, but also kneels (Luke 22:41) and falls on his face (Matt 26:39).

What kinds of "prayers" did he "pray"? Jesus prayed prayers of praise and petition—the two most basic forms of prayer in antiquity.

Praise

"Praise" includes speech to God such as "blessing" and "giving thanks."

1. *Blessing,* a donor is praised, or God's gracious favor is called down upon someone.

2. *Thanksgiving* expresses appreciation for benefits received, that is, a return to the giver. At the Last Supper, Jesus "blessed" the bread (i.e., praised Israel's Father and Patron): "He took bread, blessed it, broke it and said . . ." (Mark 14:23; Matt 27:26). Conversely, he "gave thanks" over the cup (Luke 22:17, 19; John 6:11, 23). In practice, these two words seem interchangeable for the evangelists, since Jesus' action at the feeding of the multitudes is expressed by both words: he "blessed" bread in Matt 15:36 and Mark 8:6, but "gave thanks" over loaves in Matt 14:19 and Mark 6:41.

Other types of "prayer" include the following:

Praise and Petition

Sometimes Jesus prayed prayers of "praise," as when he respectfully addressed his "Father, Lord of heaven and earth" (Matt 11:25; Luke 10:21). He prayed prayers of "petition," as when he prayed in the Garden that "God take from him the cup of bitterness" (Mark 14:36) and when he prayed for Peter (Luke 22:32). "Praise" includes psalms which affirm God's powerful deeds, confess his worth, celebrate his virtues, etc. At the Passover, diners sang the Hallel psalms, prayers of praise.

Good and Bad Prayers

In his Sermon, Jesus taught his disciples to pray "good" prayers: "pray for those who persecute you" (Matt 5:44); "whenever you pray, go into your room . . . pray to your Father in secret" (Matt 6:6, 9). Jesus also identified "bad" prayer: "When you are praying, do not heap up empty phrases as the Gentiles do; for they think that they will be heard because of their many words" (Matt 6:7). In another place he contrasts "good" and "bad" prayers:

> Two men went up to the temple to pray, one a Pharisee and the other a tax-collector. The Pharisee, standing by himself, was praying thus, "God, I thank you that I am not like other people: thieves, rogues, adulterers, or even like this tax-collector. I fast twice a week; I give a tenth of all my income." But the tax-collector, standing far off, would not even look up to heaven, but was beating his breast and saying, "God, be merciful to me, a sinner!" I tell you, this man went down to his home justified rather than the other."
> (Luke 18:9–14)

How to Pray

Jesus preached perseverance in prayer to others, and modeled it in his own prayer in the Garden. Moreover, he praised both a man who persevered in asking for bread to feed a traveler (Luke 11:5) and a woman who hounded a judge to give her justice (Luke 18:3). He himself persevered in prayer in the Garden, when he prayed his prayer three times, "Father, take this cup from me . . ." (Mark 14:36).

Posture, Gestures and Voice

Jesus himself "lifted up his eyes to heaven" as he blessed bread (Matt 14:19; Mark 6:41); he also knelt down to pray (Luke 22:41) and he fell on his face to pray (Matt 26:39). Ordinarily, Jesus stood when he prayed. There is a summary statement about Jesus praying in Hebrews that is worth noting simply because it presents Jesus praying out loud: "In the days of his flesh, Jesus offered up prayers and supplications, with loud cries and tears, to the one who was able to save him from death" (5:7).

How did Jesus come to know all of these types of prayer? The postures for them? *He was taught them.* This does not preclude his adaptation of them to his own personality and sense of his role, but it would be hard to identify any single prayer that was unique to him. On the one hand, texts such as the prayers and psalms he learned were handed on as fixed pieces of sacred speech; but we must allow that Jesus' understanding of his role and status permitted him to emphasize certain themes and employ distinctive terminology. We find no criticism of how he prayed, albeit he was criticized about so much of his words and deeds. The "Jewishness" of Jesus has been examined with the result that his words, speech, and themes are just that, "Jewish," the stuff of "high culture."

Those trying to make an imaginative scenario of Jesus learning to pray and praying certain prayers are urged to consider the materials just mentioned as foods on a buffet table. It is expected that one contemplating Jesus would select from the gospels a time, a place, a mode of prayer, a posture and some gestures mentioned in the gospels. Imagine Jesus before sunrise in a "deserted" place or at midnight on a mountain. Dial "warm" or "cool," so long as it is "dry." Just slow down to hear what Jesus says to God. Don't forget that he praises God as well as petitions him (any doxology will do, but this is a worthy one: "To the only God our Savior, through Jesus Christ our Lord, be glory, majesty, power, and authority, before all time and now and for ever. Amen" (Jude 25).

Contemplation 2: The Classic Prayer of Israel: "The Eighteen Benedictions"

There is one particular prayer, *The Eighteen Benedictions"* (a.k.a. *The Amidah*) which either in whole or in part was prayed every day. It may contain eighteen blessings, which makes it rather long for our task, and so we will make selection of certain parts that seem pertinent to our inquiry about how Jesus learned to pray. We want to look closely at this prayer for several reasons: 1. the form and cadence of each blessing; 2. familiarity with the Israelite way of talking about "holy" topics; 3. focus on certain themes repeatedly prayed: God's "name," "kingdom," and "will." It may be that Jesus did not pray all eighteen of the blessings, but their content was the stuff of Israel's praise of and petition to God. The following selections keep the number given them in the full text of the prayer.

1. **The God of History**: Blessed are you, O Lord our God and God of our fathers, the God of Abraham, the God of Isaac and the God of Jacob, the great, mighty and revered God, the Most High God who bestows loving-kindness, the creator of all things, who remembers the good deeds of the patriarchs and in love will bring a redeemer to their children's children for his name's sake. O king, helper, savior, and shield. Blessed are you, O Lord, the shield of Abraham.

2. **The God of Creation**: O Lord, are mighty forever, you revive the dead, you have the power to save. You sustain the living with loving-kindness, you revive the dead with great mercy, you support the falling, heal the sick, set free the bound, and keep faith with those who sleep in the dust. Who is like you, O doer of mighty acts? Who resembles you, a king who puts to death and restores to life and causes salvation to flourish? And you are certain to revive the dead. Blessed are you, O Lord, who revives the dead.

3. **Sanctification of God**: We will sanctify your name in this world just as it is sanctified in the highest heavens, as it is written by your prophet: "And they call out to one another and say: 'Holy, holy, holy is the LORD of hosts; the whole earth is full of his glory'" (Isa 6:3). "Blessed be the Presence of the LORD in his place" (Ezek 3:12). And in your Holy Words it is written, saying, "The LORD reigns forever, your God, O Zion, throughout all generations. Hallelujah" (Ps 146:10). Throughout all generations we will declare your greatness, and to all eternity we will proclaim your holiness. Your praise, O our God, shall never depart from our mouth, for you are a great and holy God and King. Blessed are you, O Lord, the holy God. You are holy, and your name is holy, and holy beings praise you daily. Blessed are you, O Lord, the holy God.

6. **For Forgiveness**: Forgive us, O our Father, for we have sinned; pardon us, O our King, for we have transgressed; for you pardon and forgive. Blessed are you, O Lord, who is merciful and always ready to forgive.

9. **For Deliverance from Want**: Bless this year for us, O Lord our God, together with all the varieties of its produce, for our welfare. Bestow a blessing upon the face of the earth. Satisfy us with your goodness, and bless our year like the best of years. Blessed are you, O Lord, who blesses the years.

16. **For the Answering of Prayer**: Hear our voice, O Lord our God; spare us and have pity on us. Accept our prayer in mercy and with favor, for you are a God who hears prayers and supplications. O our King, do not turn us away from your presence empty-handed, for you hear the prayers of your people Israel with compassion. Blessed are you, O Lord, who hears prayer.

The danger of my selection is that it represents just that, my particular interests, which will never be identical to yours. But these are chosen because we see in them traditional expressions of praise and petition that probably influenced Jesus, even to the point of providing some substance to his prayer, the "Our Father."

At the risk of simplifying matters, I have chosen and highlighted certain themes and phrases which have a particular resonance with Jesus' "Our Father."

Cameo 29: *Thematic Extracts from "The Eighteen Blessings"*

1. *Language of Praise and Honor*: "Declare Your praise; Blessed are You, Lord our God and God of our fathers, Isaac and Jacob; We will hallow and adore You; 'Holy, holy, holy is the Lord of hosts . . . Blessed be the glory of the Lord from its place.'"
2. *Praise of God's premier attribute, Power*, which surpasses that of any other god or storm or earthquake. "You are mighty forever . . . You resurrect the dead; You are powerful to save. You sustain the living with loving kindness, resurrect the dead with great mercy, support the falling, heal the sick, release those bound . . . Who is like You, mighty One!"
3. *Mercy and healing*: "And who can be compared to You, King, who brings death and restores life, and causes deliverance to spring forth . . . who revives the dead . . . who resurrect the dead with great mercy, support the falling, heal the sick, release those bound."
4. *Compassion*: "Hear our voice, Lord our God; merciful Father, have compassion upon us and accept our prayers in mercy and favor, for You are God who hears prayers and supplications; do not turn us away empty-handed from You, our King, for You hear the prayer of everyone. Blessed are You Lord, who hears prayer."

One might stop and imagine an Israelite praying this prayer. Begin by considering that it was said by a group, at least once a day, probably in the compound of the extended family, and recited by all. Imagine them standing erect, perhaps with their faces to the sky, and possibly their hands raised up. Look at their faces, catch the features, and pay special attention to their eyes. When you hear each speaking, are they rushing through the prayer, are there parts that they stress and say loudly? Are they attentive or does their mind wander? Real people are praying a real prayer in a real context.

A second imaginative scenario might consider how Jesus was taught this prayer and how, because of its repetition, certain remarks about God become highlighted with him. How attentive is Jesus when he prays? What does he stress? What catches his fancy (it probably changed from day to day)? Does he smile? Is he rushing or savoring the prayer? You might ask him personally what parts of the prayer are his favorites? Why?

The next contemplation will begin a careful reading of Jesus' own prayer, the "Our Father." We hope that when we begin considering the praise and petitions in that prayer we can still hear in our memory phrases and themes from the "Eighteen Blessings," which are most likely the places to start in trying to unpack the prayer of Jesus. Especially important are

Jesus' emphasis on God's "name," "kingdom," and "will," stressed in the "Eighteen Blessings." Since peasants prayed the "Eighteen Blessings" and will pray the "Our Father," keep listening for their peasant concerns in the following prayer.

Contemplation 3: Praise of God Who Is Father

As we begin to imagine Jesus teaching his signature prayer, we start with the first words, an address to "Our Father." This address of God as "Father," once rare in the Torah, becomes common in Israel's literature that is dated around the time of Jesus. So we should not be surprised to learn that Jesus, like many of his peers, addressed his God as "Father." This would not seem odd. And, no, it does not mean "Daddy," for Israelite males never had such a benevolent relationship to their fathers, as "Daddy" suggests. "Father" was a role to be respected ("Honor your father . . ."), but it has become "sacred," that is, special to Jesus, because this "Father" twice declared Jesus His "Beloved Son, with whom I am well pleased" (Mark 1:11 and 9:7). It may be tempting to see much in this; but many different types of Israelites had been called "Son of God," such as Adam (Luke 3:38), Israel's king (2 Sam 7:14), and wise and righteous men (Wis 2:12, 17; 5:5). Moreover, many persons in the Scriptures were called "beloved son" (Gen 22:2, 12, 16). Still, "Father" was Jesus' preferred reverential address. This, then, gives those imagining Jesus teaching his own prayer some particular content to put into the address of God as "Our Father." He teaches what he deeply knows and feels.

Contemplation 4: Honoring God's Name

It seems probable that Jesus often prayed the Qiddush prayer, which contains many of the terms and ideas of Jesus' own prayer. While our task is not to track down the sources of Jesus' prayer, the Qiddush, like the Amidah, was a familiar expression of praise of God, especially God's name, kingdom, and will:

> May the great Name of God be exalted and sanctified,
> throughout the world, which he has created according to his will.
> May his Kingship be established in your lifetime and in your days,
> in the lifetime of the entire household of Israel, swiftly and in the near future. May his great name be blessed, forever and ever.

> Blessed, praised, glorified, exalted, extolled, honored elevated and lauded be the Name of the holy one.
>
> Blessed is he—above and beyond any blessings and hymns, praises and consolations which are uttered in the world. Amen.
>
> May there be abundant peace from Heaven upon us and upon all Israel. Amen.

Many people find a strong correlation between this prayer and the first half of Jesus' prayer, which celebrates three aspects of God: "name," "kingdom," and "will." Jesus, moreover, is either *petitioning* God to act on His own behalf in making Himself acknowledged, or he is *praising* God, by acclaiming God's Name as unique, God's Kingdom a paradise, and God's Will as the way to walk. If petitionary, then they sound very much like the military exhortation to "Be all that you can be." God, show yourself! What does Jesus mean by these first three remarks to God? If *praising* God, then these are common and traditional ways of showing respect to God. What did his audience understand by "Keeping the Name Holy" (Exod 20:7)?

Whether we consider the absolute "Name" of God or a specific name, we can learn much from a "high context" approach to this. Traditionally, one's "name" served many purposes. A name expressed familial affinity (John*son*, Robert*son*; *Mac*Duff is Duff's son; *Fitz*patrick is Patrick's son)—that is, blood lines or pedigree, which enriches what was meant by naming God "Father." It also announced one's role in society, namely, one's trade or craft (Joe "Tailor," Phil "Glazer," Alex "Cooper"), so that any specific name used to identify God proclaimed God as Creator, Protector, Shepherd, King, and the like. In a "high context" cultural environment, it seems that the more names the better, so God could be called "Many-named."

The Commandment in Exod 20:7 demands that in general all honor God's "Name" in general and specifically. In the "Eighteen Blessings," the "Name" is identified abstractly three times: "Blessed are You who brings a redeemer . . . *for the sake of His Name* . . . Praise the Lord. You are holy and *Your Name is holy* . . . Redeem us speedily *for the sake of Your Name*." Jesus, of course, was taught this traditional reverence for God's "Name." But in the "Eighteen Blessings" we can find particular names to be honored, such as:

1. "Lord our God and God of our fathers, God of Abraham, God of Isaac and God of Jacob, the great, mighty and awesome God, exalted God . . ."

2. "King who desires life . . ."; "O King, a helper, a savior and a shield. Blessed are You Lord, Shield of Abraham. . . ," "Who can be compared to You, King, who brings death and restores life . . ."; "You, Almighty King, are a faithful and merciful healer. Blessed are You Lord, who heals the sick of His people Israel."

3. Redeemer: "Blessed are You, Lord, gracious One who pardons abundantly. Blessed are You Lord, Redeemer of Israel . . ."; "You are a generous God."

Thus God's "name" does not tell us his pedigree (God has no beginning), but instead contains information about God's "job," Patron-of-Patrons to Abraham and his sons and to David and his sons. It also expresses God's signature actions, such as "healer," shield," "redeemer," and the like. Instead of guessing, let us take a clue from the prayer Jesus was taught that he made holy God's "Name" and names. God's Name, moreover, establishes a relation with those praying, indicating favor and grace to specific mortals, as in "God of our fathers, God of Abraham, God of Isaac and God of Jacob," "Shield of Abraham," and "Redeemer of Israel." Later, disciples will acclaim that God has "the Name of Names" ("King of Kings and Lord of Lords," Deut 10:17; 1 Tim 6:15; Rev 17:14), indicating its nobility and uniqueness.

Do we imagine Jesus speaking in a special voice when he addresses the "name" of God? Does he bow? Imagine, moreover, how Jesus actually shares this reverence and relationship with others, who were not declared "Beloved Sons." Does Jesus consider the "Name" to express a special relationship with him as was stated in the phrase, "God of our fathers, God of Abraham, God of Isaac and God of Jacob" (Matt 8:11; 22:32)? Jesus, of course, is a special son. But are his disciples special also? If deeds give content to God's name, then fast forward to the four petitions in the second half of the prayer. What does Jesus want "the Name" to do?

Contemplation 5: Praising God's Kingdom

Although the term "kingdom" does not appear in "The Eighteen Blessings," in his own parables and sayings Jesus was particularly attached to "kingdom": "The Kingdom of God is at hand . . . The Kingdom of Heaven is like . . ." Again, what counts for us is what this "King" is described as doing. If Israel's king was supposed to bring peace and prosperity to the kingdom of Israel, all the more did the success of the Davidic king mirror the bounty and blessing of the heavenly King. "The Eighteen Blessings" emphatically celebrated God as "King" in this manner: 1. the heavenly King "brings death and restores life" and ". . . causes deliverance to spring forth . . . draw us near, our King, to Your service . . ." 2. "for You, Almighty *King,* are a faithful and merciful healer . . . heals the sick of His people Israel." 3. the heavenly *King,* moreover, is rich in mercy and compassion, which as Father and Benefactor of Israel, it is his pleasure to bestow abundantly: "Hear our voice, Lord our God; merciful Father, have compassion upon us and accept our prayers in mercy and favor, for You are God who hears prayers and supplications; do not turn us away empty-handed from You, our *King,* for You hear the prayer of everyone." 4. the heavenly *King* gives food and drink to the people of Israel: "Bless for us, Lord our God, this year and all the varieties of its produce for good; and bestow blessing upon the face of the earth. Satisfy us from Your bounty and bless our year like other good years, for blessing; for You are a generous God who bestows goodness and blesses the years." Does the title "king" when referring to Herod or one of his sons demand the same respect? To Caesar? Are Jesus' King and God's Kingdom of any practical use for the peasant audience?

The blessings of the heavenly King are the stuff of Jesus' signs and wonders: God has given him power to multiply food, heal diseases, silence storms, raise the dead, etc. Many people attest this by offering praise to Jesus' God after a sign or wonder performed by Jesus, such as: "He regained his sight and followed him, glorifying God; and all the people, when they saw it, praised God" (Luke 18:43; see also Luke 13:13).

If one stops here to imagine a scenario of Jesus speaking about God's "kingdom," one might decide first if he is speaking about an imaginary and ideal reign of God in general or about a particular reign of God, which brings freedom from foreign occupation, healing of all injustice, and the establishment of respectful relations between all persons, irrespective of wealth or status? Is the kingdom that of the philosopher or the peasant? Furthermore, one might just return to the parables of Jesus, where the protagonists act in hyperbolic excess, to call attention to the "Kingdom of God" in which the lead actor upsets the wisdom and power of the world, even that of peasants. In the kingdom of Jesus' Father, blessings abundantly flow from God, but no tax and tribute flow upward to the King's coffers. Moreover, when disciples are perfect, they are "merciful as your heavenly Father is merciful."

Contemplation 6: Honoring God's Will

The "Will" of God is as large as creation and as specific as the life of Jesus. All of the commands issued in Genesis 1 are examples of the will of God. At the Bible's end, the heavenly court sings the praises of God for that first creation: "Worthy are You, our Lord and God, to receive glory and honor and power, for you created all things, and by your will they existed and were created." (Rev 4:11). Moreover, God's "plan/will in Christ" refers to the time between creation and conclusion, which is also part of God's tapestry for the world: "He destined us for adoption as his children through Jesus Christ, according to the good pleasure of his will; with all wisdom and insight he has made known to us the mystery of his will, according to his good pleasure that he set forth in Christ, as a plan for the fullness of time, to gather up all things in him, things in heaven and things on earth" (Eph 1:5–11). More specifically, Jesus came "to do the will of my Father" (John 4:34; 5:30; 6:38–40), which "will" was to enlighten, give life, and heal. But God's will for Jesus himself is more narrowly described: "The Son of Man *must* be mocked and murdered," which Jesus explicitly tells Peter represents the thoughts of God (Mark 8:34). This "will" is most on display in the Garden ("Remove this cup from me; yet, not what I want, but what you want," Mark 14:36). In regard to Jesus' disciples, the "will" of God is similar: "For it is God's will that by doing right you should silence the ignorance of the foolish" (1 Pet 2:15) and "It is better to suffer for doing good, if suffering should be God's will, than to suffer for doing evil" (1 Pet 3:17; 4:19). Finally the will of God is behavior which honors God: "Let your light shine before others, so that they may see your good works and give glory to your Father in heaven" (Matt 5:16; 1 Pet 2:12).

Here might be a good spot to pause and imagine Jesus and his remark about the "will of God." We can imagine him discoursing about this will in general and what it means for him in particular. What does his face look like when he tells the disciples that he "must" go to Jerusalem to be mocked to death, but then vindicated by the same God who sent him? This is, as the Godfather said, "Personal," for he is fully invested in it. How does he react when Peter tells him how foolish this sounds? What is he telling Peter when he says that Peter thinks the thoughts of the masses but not the thoughts of God? Does talking about the "will of God" make him sad or glad?

Contemplation 7: Give Us Today Our Daily Bread

Thus far, we imagine Jesus addressing a crowd of peasant farmers who are intensely focused on the perennial problems that farmers face: rain or drought, enough seed to sow, favorable growing conditions, and a successful harvest. It has been noted that when the gospel says that the crowds whom Jesus fed "ate their fill," that remark likely reflects immediate food insufficiency which regularly threatened Jesus' audience. They never "ate their fill," because they had to ration grain from harvest to harvest. One might plan for the Passover feast or a wedding or some other festival, but there was not much leeway over food stores. Return to *Cameo 6: What's for Lunch?* to visualize what this looked like. So, we should imagine that Jesus is talking about real bread, the staff of life, which was at least a half of one's daily caloric intake. Jesus himself seems privileged to be fed by various people, starting with Peter, then a tax collector, even Pharisees, and eventually dear friends like Martha, Mary, and Lazarus. Often his disciples were invited as well to eat what they had not planned for. But this hardly clouds the naked fact of food insufficiency which constantly threatened Israel. The following cameo will help those contemplating food insufficiency to appreciate the frequency and severity of droughts and famines, which make Jesus' words about "daily bread" much more than vague wishes.

Cameo 30: Rains (Maybe), Droughts, and Famines

Rains, which came only in the winter months, sporadically and skimpily, were called "the early rains and the late rains." Although Jerusalem might receive abundant rain, the Galilee did not (10" per annum in Tiberius). And the rains were unpredictable, often not coming at all, which created droughts that might last one, three, or seven years. But the truth is, "There were many widows in Israel in the time of Elijah, when the heaven was shut up for three years and six months, and there was a severe famine over all the land" (Luke 4:25), or "Now Elisha had said to the woman . . . 'Get up and go with your household, and settle wherever you can; for the Lord has called for a famine, and it will come on the land for seven years'" (2 Kgs 8:1). If drought, then famine that devastated villages, towns, cities, and lands alike. Genesis reports famine in the time of Abraham (Gen 12:10), Isaac (Gen 26:1) and Jacob (". . . and the seven years of famine began to come, just as Joseph had said. There was famine in every country," Gen 41:54). One particular famine occurred under Claudius (41–54 CE), which was noted in Acts 11:28: "Agabus predicted that there would be a severe famine over all the world; and this took place during the reign of Claudius." Josephus, the historian of Israel, told a story about this famine: "Her arrival (Queen Helena of Adiabene) was very advantageous to the people of Jerusalem; for a famine oppressed them at that time, and many people died for want of money to procure food. Queen Helena sent servants to Alexandria to buy a great quantity of grain, and others to Cyprus to bring back dried figs. They quickly returned with the provisions, which she immediately distributed to those in need . . . and when her son Izates was informed of this famine, he sent great sums of money to the principal men in Jerusalem." Jerusalem, yes. But was there any relief for the peasant villages in Galilee?

If one decides to contemplate Jesus speaking these words, it might help to recall some of his remarks about abundance (rare) and insufficiency (common). The abundant harvest in Luke 12:15–21 should have been shared with the neighbors, and thus the recipient of the windfall harvest would be "rich with God." Remember the insufficiency of wine at the Cana wedding feast. Recall Jesus' exhortation to a husband and wife to trust in God's bounty, even as they have no land to farm or wool to weave (Matt 6:25–33)—radical insufficiency. Thousands of hungry people, who have immediate insufficiency of food to return home, are fed until filled, proof of which is seen in seven or twelve baskets of leftover bread (Mark 6:33–44; and 8:1–9). Droughts and famines, so common in Jesus' time, ravage our world today. So as one imagines Jesus teaching his disciples to beg from

God real bread, remember that he honored the foolish who "fed the hungry," so begging bread is joined with giving bread, just as it was with Jesus.

Contemplation 8: Forgive Us Our Debts

Although our liturgical version reads, "Forgive us our trespasses," the earliest version of the prayer petitioned, "Forgive us our debts." Back in chapter 4, there was a cameo on taxes, tax collectors, and debt which you might want to re-visit. The vast weight of evidence from Galilee at this time indicates that peasants were always in debt and very seriously so. The Roman system of taxes showed no mercy, and so farmer after farmer, especially in drought and famine, borrowed to pay the taxes, eventually finding their farms "under water," as was the case with mortgaged houses in the recent crisis. Elites never pay taxes (what's new?), so that the burden of taxation fell on peasant farmers. Consider the bizarre largess of the Greek king who canceled taxes:

> (Demetrius to the Jews) "I free you and exempt all the Jews from payment of tribute and salt tax and crown levies, and instead of collecting the third of the grain and the half of the fruit of the trees that I should receive, I release them from this day and henceforth. I will not collect them from the land of Judah or from the three districts added to it from Samaria and Galilee, from this day and for all time. And let Jerusalem and her environs, her tithes and her revenues, be holy and free from tax." (1 Macc 10:29–31)

No taxes whatsoever, and *not* the third of the grain, *nor* half of the fruit of the trees either? Those peasants breathed easily, for a while, but not so the peasants of Jesus' time. Historians inform us that farms in Galilee were being expropriated by debt to such a great extent, that the tax revenue from idle land plummeted, which disturbed even the Romans. Emperor Tiberius is said to have commented to those buying the contracts to collect taxes: "Remember, we are there to sheer the sheep, not to skin them." "Forgive us our debts," then, is a guttural petition for Jesus' peasant audience, just as was "give us daily bread."

One way to imagine a scenario on this topic is to refer back to Jesus' parables that have to do with debt and debt forgiveness. He told a parable to his host at dinner about a man with two debtors (Luke 7:41–43). A man with debtors is a very ordinary event, but what this creditor does with the debts is not: he forgave debts of 500 denarii and 50. *Nobody forgives debts, but nobody!* Again, Jesus told a parable about a rich man calling in his debts, only to find that his greatest debtor (10,000 talents) could not repay it. At first the rich man does what rich people did in Jesus' world: he defends his honor by ordering the debtor, his wife, and family to be sold into slavery in payment of the debt. How ordinary, nothing at all strange here. But when the debtor asks for "debt relief," the creditor incredibly rescinds the order to sell the debtor into slavery and actually "cancels the debt" (Matt 18:27). This action is the hyperbolic, over-the-top, zany action that makes the parable listeners howl with laughter, because it is so inconceivable. But that is the point: debt, enormous debt, is simply canceled, at least in God's world. Might this fantasy action have ever happen in the lives of Jesus' peasant audience?

Ideally, an individual peasant might cancel the debt a neighbor owed him—as crazy as this sounds. Or, one might burn down the place where debt records were kept, as happened thirty years after Jesus' death: "The victors burst into the palaces of Agrippa and Bernice; they next carried their combustibles to the public archives, eager to destroy the money-lenders' bonds and to prevent the recovery of debts . . . to cause a rising of the poor against the rich, sure of impunity" (Josephus, *Jewish War* 2.426–427). Please imagine Jesus speaking this petition to peasant farmers, who either themselves, their neighbors, or their relatives, were hopelessly in debt. The penalties for failure to pay debt were severe, such as slavery, prison, and the like (Matt 18:30; 25:39). Jesus, a peasant, speaks honestly to the immediate concerns of fellow peasants. Real "bread" and actual "debt."

Contemplation 9: Lead Us Not into Temptation

If the default of our modern imagination is to read this as "temptation" to sin, please allow a more realistic possibility to enter. "Daily bread" and "debt forgiveness" are specific and real petitions for actual peasant farmers. Push the story one mile further: what would happen to a debtor who could not repay debts? He would be taken before an authority and be officially dispossessed of his land. Instead of "temptation," read "trial," as in a *judicial trial*, that is, a *legal proceeding* whereby the peasant's land is publicly and irrevocably forfeited to his creditor (the first meaning of the Greek word, *peirasmos,* is judicial trial and only by metaphor extends to moral trials). A peasant's hope was to avoid ever coming to such a "trial" where his land would be seized. The "trial," therefore, which peasants faced, was not a moral "testing" at all ("like gold tested in fire"), but an economic disaster. They are not perfected in this crisis but made landless, begging poor, reduced to tenancy, and worse. This is not about virtue, but a tsunami of woe—landlessness. Jesus apparently was landless, whether because his family owned no land to begin with or it was seized in debt repayment. He knew many who had been stripped of their land because of debt, and this was done legally and instantaneously at a "trial" before a magistrate.

If one is inclined to construct an imaginative scenario of Jesus teaching this part of his prayer to his fellow peasants, keep it real. See Jesus addressing the paramount need of his fellow peasants: land which yields food. His tone is careful, compassionate, and sharp. He does not smile when he says these words, but grieves to see the destruction of lives resulting from being "brought to trial." Does Jesus have any remedy for this economic crisis? Can he count on "debt forgiveness" among the money lenders? What does he expect God to do? What might be his feelings (remember his "gut reaction" to illness)?

Contemplation 10: But Deliver Us from the Evil One

Once more, our default understanding is to generalize this petition so as to make it a prayer to resist all evil, everywhere, in all forms. But when Jesus continues to address his peasant farmer audience, this petition would naturally lead his hearers to finish the story of debt and land confiscation by imagining the "Evil One" as the premier evil feared in the lives of all peasants, the Tax Collector. We pay our taxes voluntarily by sending our moneys to the IRS; but peasants were confronted by armed men who came to them and physically extracted the taxes owed. We know that remarkably detailed tax records were kept, indicating that a certain peasant payed "y" tax last year, but this year he has had a good harvest and his ewes birthed two lambs, and, as this is recorded, larger taxes are assessed this year—on the spot. The armed men literally take the taxes in kind (grain, oil, etc.) and carry them away. Although a thief may come at night, these tax collectors arrive in daylight with no surprise. They collect the taxes they assessed, then and there. No discussion, no amelioration, no mercy! The Tax Collector at the gate is the person most feared by all peasants; without discussion, he is "the Evil One" from whom peasants desperately pray to escape.

Although the gospels never record an event such as just described, we can easily see the effects of brutal tax collecting. Jesus speaks about day-laborers, men without land who hire themselves out for wages (Matt 20:1–16). It does not take much imagination to ask why they are landless and reduced to day labor. Jesus also talks about tenant farmers who contracted to tend a rich man's vineyard (Mark 12:1–8). In the logic of the parable, the rich absentee landlord would be "The Evil One" who wants his produce, which the tenants refuse to surrender. The owner who hired the day laborers is indeed exceedingly foolish to pay all workers the same wage; he is hardly "the Evil One" here, although incredibly unwise with his money. The absentee landlord, however, acts in peasant eyes as "the Evil One," who takes from the tenants—not taxes, but the product of their labor. Finally, recall how Jesus shocked his audiences by talking about "debt cancellation," not tax collection. How strange this would sound to peasants, who only knew of tax collection and considered debt cancellation an impossible event. They all knew who "the Evil One" was.

So, in imagining a scenario for Jesus' speaking this fourth petition, scan all of the faces of the peasants listening to Jesus. Every single one of them has faced the tax police who annually extract taxes in kind, that is, carry off grain, fruits, oil, animals, etc. Every eye has seen and every ear has heard the horror stories, not simply of the harvest confiscated, but the unfeeling, abusive, humiliating shame inflicted on defenseless peasants. See in the faces of Jesus' audience their resonance with his petition. Everyone prays for this.

Contemplation 11: Watching Jesus Pray His Own Prayer (Mark 14:32–42)

Back in chapter four, we imagined Jesus praying in the Garden. With your permission, we repeat that contemplation for the simple reason that Jesus not only taught a prayer (the "Our Father"), but prayed it himself. He modeled for his disciples his own prayer, both in terms of its content and in instructions how to pray it.

Jesus does not intend to be alone when he prays in the Garden, but that is what happens. If all disciples near and far are asleep, then who knew what the text of Jesus' prayer was? Since Jesus is so often presented as modeling what he taught his disciples, then it is not surprising that the evangelists provide an appropriate text for this prayer, namely, the very prayer that Jesus taught them earlier. His posture is not eccentric ("He threw himself flat on the ground"); nor is his delivery bizarre. He speaks with the intensity of feeling which was a regular part of his speech, an intensity sharpened because he reveals his intense relationship with his Father, who called him his "Beloved Son."

If readers are imagining an appropriate scenario of this episode, they are more immediate to the scene than the disciples were. Granted that the evangelists do not repeat the entire text of Jesus' prayer, but highlight only the appropriate petition to God and his reverent honoring of his Father. "Abba, Father, for you all things are possible; remove this cup from me; yet, not what I want, but what you want" (Mark 14:36, words repeated in Matt 26:39 and John 18:11). Looking more closely, what does Mark want us to see beside the fact that Jesus prayed? What does this sound like? Silent words, whispered words? Is his face downward? Look at his eyes. Besides the text he prayed, he illustrates something very significant by praying this prayer *three times*. The repetition is not because he did not get it right the first time, but because he exemplifies his own teaching of perseverance in prayer (Luke 11:5–8; 18:2–5).

Here Jesus prays the two common forms of prayer: first, he *petitions* God to "remove this cup from me," but balances it with a declaration of *honor and respect*, "not what I want, but what you want." His persevering loyalty to God contrasts with the failure of the sleeping disciples, who could not persevere, i.e., "watch one hour" (remember they drank four cups of wine at Supper, while Jesus fasted). His face eventually becomes serene, not sad; he swells with confidence, not fear. He voluntarily accepts his fate, a mark of courage and nobility. His aloneness will shortly be complete when all the disciples flee and leave Jesus alone. See him stand, walk over to the sleeping three and rouse them. See all four of them go out to meet the soldiers. He willingly begins to drink "the cup"; he profoundly honors his Father in doing this.

Contemplation 12: Jesus' Final Prayer

If it is appropriate to repeat Jesus' prayer in the Garden, then it is also desirable that we repeat Jesus' last prayer, when he prayed Psalm 22. First of all, in a "high context" setting, the disciples of Jesus may be presumed to know by heart the psalms or at least recognize them. They would know what kind of psalm Jesus is praying when he says, "My God, my God . . ." (Ps 22:1). The form of the psalm has many twins in the Psalter, psalms that begin with a question asked of God, which is properly a complaint:

"Why, O LORD, do you stand far off? Why do you hide in times of trouble?" (Ps 10:1)

"Why do you hide your face? Why do you forget our affliction?" (Ps 44:24)

"Why do you hide your face? Why do you forget our affliction and oppression?" (Ps 74:1)

"Why should the nations say, 'Where is their God?'" (Ps 79:10)

Yes, there was a type of psalm known as a prayer of "complaint" (or as one scholar said, "Yes, you may whine to God"). Those hearing Jesus' words would know immediately what kind of psalm this is: "My God, my God, why have you forsaken me?" They know that it expresses in a stereotypical fashion an address to God in which the person praying demands to know his status with God. It is, moreover, a psalm of praise as well as of petition.

Prayers all have purposes: why does so-and-so say this-and-that to such a person, *for what purpose*? If only the first line of the psalm is considered, there is a remote possibility that the person praying is abusing God, but only a very, very remote possibility. Rather, when the whole psalm is considered, Psalm 22 becomes a profound expression of faith in God (honor) and a petition for God's help (also honor).

This becomes clear only when the whole text of the psalm is considered, and not just its opening line. Since we know the type of psalm, let us now investigate its contents, that is, all that is stated in it. Psalm 22 is structured in three parts, each part first declaring the acute distress of the person praying, which is balanced by a powerful expression of faith, thus thrice producing this antiphonal rhythm: "distress/loyalty . . . worse distress/greater loyalty . . . and maximum distress/ profound loyalty."

22:1 *My God, my God, why have you forsaken me?* Why are you so far from helping me, from the words of my groaning? 22:2 O my God, I cry by day, but you do not answer; and by night, but find no rest.	22:3 Yet you are holy, enthroned on the *praises* of Israel. 22:4 In you our ancestors *trusted*; they *trusted*, and you *delivered* them. 22:5 To you they cried, and *were saved*; in you they *trusted*, and were *not put to shame*.

The situation is wretched, especially because the afflicted person prays constantly but finds no comfort. Yet his faith is indeed strong, especially in the face of fearful terror. He comes from *good stock*, "his ancestors *trusted . . . trusted* and were *delivered*; they *cried* and were *saved . . .* they were *not put to shame*." He, then, was raised in a house of faith and he himself is a chip off the old block. He claims the same faith as his ancestors.

22:6 But I am a worm, and not human; *scorned* by others, and *despised* by the people. 22:7 All who see me *mock at me; they make mouths at me, they shake their heads;* 22:8 "Commit your cause to the LORD; *let him deliver him—let him rescue the one in whom he delights!"*	22:9 Yet it was you who *took me from the womb*; you *kept me safe* on my mother's breast. 22:10 On you I was cast from my birth, and since my mother bore me *you have been my God.* 22:11 Do not be far from me, for trouble is near and there is no one to help.

Not only did his ancestors trust God, but the one praying the psalm claims that he too has been very close to God and has previously known God's favor, from the womb and from his mother's breast. God hallowed his life's beginning: "since my birth, you have been my God." Based on this personal favor, he appeals for God to remain faithful to him: "Do not be far from me, for trouble is near and there is no one to help." He comes from faithful stock, and he himself is a chip off the old block.

22:12 Many bulls encircle me, strong bulls surround me; 22:13 they open wide their mouths at me, like a ravening and roaring lion . . . 22:16 Dogs are all around me; evildoers encircle me. My hands and feet have shriveled; 22:17 I can count all my bones.	22:19 But you, O LORD, *do not be far away*! O *my help, come quickly to my aid!* 22:20 *Deliver* my soul from the sword, my life from the power of the dog! 22:21 *Save* me from the mouth of the lion! From the horns of the wild oxen *rescue* me.

These are not complaints as in vv. 1–2, but petitions that are rooted in faith, certainly not despair. His petitions speed to God's throne: *"be not far away . . . come to my aid . . . deliver my soul . . . save me . . . rescue me."* If the bystanders mistook "Eli, Eli . . ." as a cry to Elijah to save him, the disciples know that Jesus spoke to God as the only, sure source of his salvation. The disciples would certainly *not* see these dying words as a loss of faith, but just the opposite. Thus a person imagining a cultural scenario will study the whole psalm and imagine how pieces of it are woven into the narrative of the crucifixion scene. Most importantly, this person will try to hear Jesus praying the whole psalm, both the dark parts and their counterbalancing confessions of faith. How, then, does the person imagining the scene view the very dying of Jesus? Is this a time to "have that mind within you which was in Christ Jesus"? (Phil 2:5).

If the reader wishes to make an imaginative scenario of this scene, please go back to *Cameo 13*, where a typical crucifixion scene is described, something all in a "high context" world would know. But use all your senses to imagine it, especially sight and hearing. Of all times, let your feelings rise to give a sense of touch to the events.

Or, one making a scenario might take the next two pieces of the narrative for a more extended contemplation, namely, the rending of the temple veil and the confession of Jesus' executioner. The gospel writers say that at the death of Jesus the temple veil was torn in two, from top to bottom. If we imagine that the front of the 90' tall temple was covered by a heavy tapestry, then the only way it could be torn in two *from top to bottom* would be by God's immediate action. The remark that the veil was torn *from top to bottom* cannot be an act of mortal strength. Moreover, the evangelists narrate that the executioner there heard what Jesus said and was profoundly moved by it: "Now when the centurion, who stood facing him, saw that in this way he breathed his last, he said, 'Truly this man was God's Son!'" (Mark 15:39). He heard what Psalm 22 says, namely, a profound trust in God, a saintly action. Hearing this from a crucified man was enough to make him reassess Jesus, not as a criminal who deserved to die, but as a holy man who suffered innocently. These observations might help us in appreciating Psalm 22 as a prayer of faith, not despair. When those imagining this final prayer of Jesus hear for themselves these words, what do they hear? How do they respond to Jesus' words? Do they agree with the executioner? See each scene and hear the rip in the curtain and the loud voice of Jesus' executioner. Imagine his voice, its volume, tone, and cadence. How does he hold his head when he speaks? Is he looking at Jesus or at his soldiers? And his face, note it before Jesus dies and after he hears the dying words. Does he feel anything about Jesus besides a revised verdict of his guilt? Is he embarrassed?

Are conclusions necessary? Possible? The possible results of seeing Jesus more closely, hearing him more accurately, and following him more nearly are not arguments for our heads. Rather, because they are imaginative reconstructions of Jesus in his own culture, they touch a part of the human experience more immediate than correct thinking. Every prelude suggested here has one aim only: to bring the person imagining Jesus closer in relationship to him. Preludes, while satisfying our minds, work when they empower the physical senses of the persons praying, inflame the mind, not only to see in technicolor but to feel alert in ones' emotions. Insofar as the scenarios actually draw those imagining into the fictive, but real presence of the human Jesus, they are successful and so valuable. By their fruits you shall know them. Amen.

Index of Topics

Index of Scripture

NEW TESTAMENT

Matthew

INDEX OF SCRIPTURE

Made in the USA
Middletown, DE
06 March 2019